bloomingdale's book of home decorating

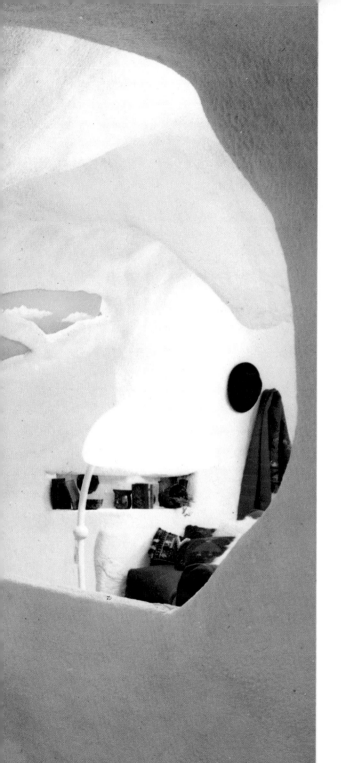

bloomingdale's book of home decorating

barbara d'arcy

harper & row, publishers
new york
evanston
san francisco
london

Thanks

Many of the photographs in this book appeared in publications that were kind enough to permit their reproduction. My appreciation to *McCalls, Ladies' Home Journal, Esquire, House & Garden, Modern Bride* and Reinhart Wolf of *Shöner Wohnen.* My thanks, too, to Richard Averill Smith, Normal McGrath, Phillip Roedell, Tom Weir and Ernest Silva for the many other room photographs that make up the body of this book.

I owe Michael A. Davenport a very warm and sincere gratitude for his infinite patience and ability to organize and put into writing the many design practices and techniques that I have worked with for years but never verbalized. Books like this don't just happen. Along with technical knowledge of content, there has to be a flair for communication. There are thousands of decisions to be made along the months of writing to have a readable flow of information. Michael and I agonized over them. And laughed over them. And the whole experience was work. But fun.

Photographs on pages 134 and 149 are from *House & Garden*, copyright © 1964, 1965, 1968, 1972 by the Condé Nast Publications, Inc. Photographs by Tom Yee.

Photographs on pages 42 and 62 reproduced by permission of *Esquire Magazine*, copyright © 1966 by Esquire, Inc.

The photograph on page 159 is reproduced by permission of *McCalls;* pages 41, 55, 57 and 114, *The Ladies' Home Journal;* pages 65 and 214, *Modern Bride;* pages 26, 79, and 144, Reinhart Wolf of *Shöner Wohnen.*

First Edition

Designed by Dorothy Schmiderer

Library of Congress Cataloging in Publication Data
D'Arcy, Barbara White.
    Bloomingdale's book of home decorating.
    1. Interior decoration. I. Bloomingdale Brothers, inc., New York. II. Title.
NK2115.D26   747'.213   73-4064
ISBN 0-06-010948-3

To my mother, Ida D'Arcy, who taught my eyes to see as a designer . . . from my very earliest days;

my brother Albert D'Arcy, who insisted that I keep my feet on the road to a design career;

my brother Paul D'Arcy, who taught me the value of research and helped me collect a vast library of irreplaceable reference books —most of them gifts. Without them—and him —I'd be absolutely lost;

my husband, Kirk White, who, because of a wide spectrum of interests, opened up new ranges of ideas and urged me to reach out in directions I had never thought of before;

and to Marvin Traub, President of Bloomingdale's, who had faith in me many, many years ago.

The above list of people is in chronological order—but without all of them equally this book could not be. Nor could I.

B. D'A.

contents

Part VI / Lighting: The Fifth Dimension

Part VII / Accessories: The Final Touches

Part VIII / Where to Go for Help

preface

More than a book about decorating, this is a book about style.

Setting out to decorate a room can be an awesome thing. I know. I've done hundreds of them—including the ones I live in. And starting is always the most difficult part.

The final goal of designing and decorating a room is to create atmosphere. And atmosphere is style. That's what *Bloomingdale's Book of Home Decorating* is all about.

Hopefully, this book will tell you how to organize your thoughts so that you can get those rooms into shape in your mind. It may even help you to think. And see. And develop taste and flair. Those are the things you apply to a room to give it atmosphere and make it a suitable background for your particular tempo and style of living.

It takes some doing. But it doesn't have to be awesome.

introduction

What Is This Thing Called Taste?

In making your home more attractive you not only provide a more enjoyable background for your family but you personally benefit and grow. But only if you put something of yourself into the job. Unfortunately, decorating has been the victim of mass production. As a result, homes all over the country have a dreadful conformity. This is something I've always tried to combat in my approach to the design and decoration of personal surroundings—to rid rooms of the drab, mass-produced look without any trace of personal expression. The absence of excitement and inspiration is too often due to the fear of doing something wrong. To lack of knowledge about what to do. And lack of gumption to give the problem time and thought—which are what it takes.

Our love and desire for beauty are instinctive. If we look back through history we can see originality in almost all cultures. Our forebears made things with their hands or directed the crafting of their furniture and silver by the local carpenter and silversmith. Though their homes were often crude, they had great charm, color and individuality.

The aim of interior design is to bring beauty, graciousness and dignity into the place where you live. It can work for you regardless of how simple your house or apartment may be.

Learn to know yourself and your family— what you do, what you would like to do and, very important, what your dreams are.

We can easily go on, year after year, without appreciating our own individuality, with-out seeing the essential differences between ourselves and others. A room that is right for your neighbor is not necessarily the room that is right for you.

Are you a conservative, home-loving person whose life centers around home and family? Then a simple, practical and comfortable traditional background is right for you. Your home should suggest great warmth.

Are you a gay, social person constantly involved ·with people? Then your home should be planned with an eye to entertaining, using gay, light colors and expressing the mood of celebration.

Perhaps books, conversation, music and art are your interests. Then let this cultural inclination be expressed in the way you decorate your home.

Or—you may be a dramatic sort of person. You may like to startle people. You take special delight in being different. For you the sky is the limit in imaginative decorating.

Perhaps you are a community leader, very active in civic affairs. Your background should be conventional, subdued, dignified and traditional—with perhaps a touch of modern. But oh-so-well balanced. Such a background builds an aura of respect and stability for you as a person.

Maybe you're involved in world travel because of your profession, and home is merely a stopping-off place between trips. Then it should be quite solid and stable but simple from the standpoint of maintenance. It should reflect your travels but should not be filled with brasses that need to be polished.

The next step in planning your personal environment is to cultivate vivid and definite reactions to everything you see and do. Learn to define your likes and dislikes. Make lists of things you like and don't like. Likes and dislikes are really what make up that thing called taste.

Personally, I enjoy an original approach to decorating. I respond to effects that are not conventional. But when you are beginning, when you're not sure of yourself, don't strain to develop some idea that is wildly different. If you do, one of two things could happen: You might never be able to make up your mind what to do, and as a result do nothing. Or, instead of arriving at something pleasing to you, you could end up with something tricky and difficult to live with.

Look through the best magazines and books. Some illustration may start your mind working and perhaps crystalize an idea. Go shopping. Look in better store windows. Study the model rooms in better department stores. Try to figure out how certain effects have been achieved. If you see something you like, try to work out the same effect. Copy it. Shamelessly. After all, a professional has worked it out and chances are it's good.

Don't be in a hurry to be original. Wait until you have developed some actual experience. For some reason, the mere doing leads to later inventiveness. It leads to confidence.

But how do you ever decide what you want to do to a room? Everyone works in a slightly different fashion. All I can do is tell you how I work on a room. Maybe you'll find a method you can use.

For most rooms you need to discover and develop a theme. You should have some idea of the character you want your room to express:

Should the room be as modern as you can make it?
Should it be bright and gay?
Should it be solid and conservative?
Should it be unorthodox and imaginative?
Should books play an important role?
Should the room be simple and dignified?
Should it be sleek and sophisticated?
Is art an important part of your life?
Are you a person in pursuit of the avant-garde?

Ask yourself questions like these—and answer them. This is the first major step in creating your room environment. Now, then, take inventory. You may already own things that will help you get started:

A piece of furniture that you can't bear to part with
A fine old painting, or an extremely modern one
A piece of modern sculpture, pre-Colombian or African art
A collection of old green Wedgwood
An Oriental rug
Some eighteenth-century fruit paintings
An unusual collection of pewter, Indian baskets, boxes, shells, minerals, anything interesting
An old quilt

I suggested earlier that you make a list of your likes and dislikes to give you a sort of blueprint of your taste. You'll see examples of my taste in the many styles of the rooms in this book, but here's a little preview—and just possibly a guide for making your own list.

I dislike: Imitation brick, phony wood paneling, pressed wood graining, plastic flowers and most lamps. I particularly hate period furniture that's not true to style—whether the furniture is original or a copy. I think one should stick to the authentic in furniture as well as architecture.

As to my likes: I like rough plaster, terra

cotta, plank floors and big baskets filled with lots of dried plants or with lots of one kind of fresh flowers. I like earthen pottery and highly polished chrome. I love four-poster beds and the way they dominate a room, enclosing space to give you a feeling of warmth and a hideaway when you want it. I like books, books, books in every room in a house. Old and new books, big art books and small books of poetry. All rooms *need* books.

I like fabric-covered walls and rooms with many levels. I like unexpected combinations of things like a Louis XV chair upholstered in men's suiting fabric, contemporary fabrics in crisp, clear colors.

Further, I like brick floors, walls partly covered with ceramic tiles, heavy moldings and seventeenth-century furniture. I'm particularly fond of long, narrow tables. Nothing, to me, can take the place of real gold leaf that is rubbed, mellowed and burnished.

Collections of things! Things that represent one viewpoint delight me: Thai buddhas, English brass tea caddies, crystal objects used solely for ornament. I like things arranged together around a lamp and held in a pool of light: A plant, a piece of sculpture, a box, an ashtray, one nut.

I like area rugs and animal skins.

And, finally, I like lavender and orange. Together.

"I Couldn't Live in a Room Like That."

I hear that hundreds of times from people viewing the model rooms at Bloomingdale's in New York.

And it's quite true. No one room is for everybody—whether it's a display room in a store or the living room of friends. A room is a re-flection of one person, one family, the way one lives.

Bloomingdale's is in the center of New York City—the world's most exciting melting pot. There are varieties of living styles within this small geographic area that stagger the imagination. Too, this is an area of unusual sophistication. That's why there has been such a great variety of styles in the model rooms I've designed over the years. They were varied because the population in our area is varied. But each room was for someone. That someone could be a typical New York East Side apartment dweller or a celebrity who lives part of the year in the south of France. I rely on all sorts of people for inspiration for the model rooms. For your room, you are the inspiration.

So often I am asked, "How do you go about doing those rooms?" Perhaps as I go through the process step by step, you'll find out how to go about doing *your* model room—the one that you'll be living in.

part 1 / easy architectural changes

1/multi-levels for many rooms

Most rooms are boxes. But you don't have to live in them that way. There are hundreds of things you can do, from the simple application of moldings to creating an architectural sculpture, like a fireplace that lends everything from dignity to amusement to a room.

Fabric can be used on walls; paint and wallpaper can do much to give a room personality. Here are some techniques that I have used many times in the little boxes at Bloomingdale's that end up as model rooms.

The Barbara D'Arcy Room. This is a room that I did for myself, part of a series of model rooms called The Creators. Because it was my room, I combined many of the elements that I truly love. It had a beamed ceiling with a range of colors that match the upholstery below. There are three elements here that work particularly well together: Brilliant, strong color, white plaster, and multi-level construction. This was primarily thought of as a studio in the country, but the multi-levels transform the studio into distinct areas for study, living and dining. Because it was my own room I felt free to mix the furniture and furnishings. With the modern conversation pit there's an antique French farm table, a country French armoire in an antique white finish (filled with all my treasures) and barely showing at the left, a modern plexiglass table.

Multi-levels. We are accustomed to think of walls when it comes to dividing space into rooms. But cubes in space can function the same way. And these are created by using multi-levels. The change of levels from one area to another provides different vistas. It's much like viewing an area from down in a valley, and again from atop a hill. The view is entirely different. One way I like to work multi-levels in a fairly good-sized room is to put the lowest point—say a conversation pit—in the middle of the room around a center of interest like a fireplace or in front of a view window. Then place one platform for dining to one side, and on another side have a third level for work or study. Here, on the left you see a table on a higher level than the seating pit, but this area has multi-levels in itself. The table is in another pit supported by a column under the great piece of black plexiglass that serves as the top. With this pit arrangement, you actually sit on the floor level with your legs dropping down into the pit—much like the arrangement you would find in a Japanese restaurant. On the far left of the table is a ledge on which one could pile masses of cushions. I chose plexiglass for the table to give a shiny, reflecting surface to contrast with the rest of the room, which is totally carpeted in a very dry, feltlike carpeting in charcoal gray. The lightness of the Noguchi lanterns also gives a lift to what could otherwise be a somber room. The table in the conversation pit is a cube of mitered black plexiglass. The upholstery of the modular units was in a woolen fabric exactly the same color as the carpeting—Oxford gray.

The Victor Vasarely Room. This multi-level stainless steel environment was designed as part of The Creators series. Vasarely is famous for working in shades and tones of one color. Because many of his works are done in brilliant colors, like whole ranges of blues and greens or yellows, I selected the most neutral color I could think of. I put together gray lacquer, stainless steel (which I consider to be gray in color), gray suede and gray carpeting so that the entire room was all in gray. The only color accent in this room was the floor to ceiling ficus tree, the asparagus sprengeri and the Vasarely work of art, which is multicolored. Although you see only two levels—the dining area and seating pit—actually there were seven levels, each with its own mood. I used multi-levels for changes of space area, still maintaining an overall feeling of openness. The dining table was a great crisscross of polished steel that contrasted with the fireplace and other elements of the room that were in brushed stainless steel. The walls and ceiling were lacquered gray to match the carpeting. All the individual banquettes were upholstered in gray suede, which contrasts beautifully with the smoothness and shine of the rest of the room. Although the room is in one color, it is not monotonous because of the contrasts in texture and the architectural excitement of the multi-levels.

The Pierre Cardin Room—another in The Creators series. This is total flight of fancy—I freely admit. Certainly this is not a room for everyone, but if you want to indulge your fantasies and can live in this sort of environment, this is one way to do it. The entire room was upholstered in a felt that looked like gray flannel. It was a two-level room, with the platform risers formed in amoeba shapes, and covered with matching gray carpeting. All of the framework you see as you look back into the room was made of baffles—the kind you see in the theatre—spaced thirty to thirty-six inches apart. Each baffle was made in a slightly different shape so that you got a series of different profiles as you looked through. The desk was upholstered in gray, too, and cantilevered from a stainless steel pole running from floor to ceiling. The seating units were in four different heights but all the same crescent shape. They were grouped together to form a seating island on which you could either stretch out or perch. The chaise longue in the background was upholstered in metallic silver snakeskin and set into the platform. The concentric shapes at the back framed the window, which was really a two-way mirror you could see out of, but which concealed an ugly view. The round plexiglass globe held a television set with all the works visible.

The Cave Room. On the title page of this book is a photo of the Cave Room. This is a detail of the dining area of that room. The legs of the dining table were white plexiglass columns lit from within. The floor was covered with tiny one-fourth-inch-square mirror (not the most practical floor covering in the world, I grant you). I am especially taken by the free form of this molded architecture, which has been practiced in the south of France for many years. This was sprayed urethane foam, but it could be done in rough plaster molded over a wire lath-and-wood frame. This dining area with its curved, molded ceiling had the feeling of a cave, and yet, because of the lightness of the table and the reflections in the mirrored floor there was nothing closed-in about it. This free-form molding of a room is most effective when in white. Colors on shapes like this are a bit much.

Two ways of treating one form of architecture. This was a very elaborate room, as you can see. I used *treillage*, the Edwardian architectural style, and made it look contemporary by creating an octagonal pavilion room with a cupola ceiling entirely lit from behind through white plexiglass. I think it's interesting to see how one room can be treated in two entirely different ways: One in all-white lacquered furniture that is Edwardian in feeling, but mixed with French steel garden furniture;

22

the other in "naturals," from the caramel-colored suede, table and chairs in an almost bleached finish, natural straw, pre-Columbian sculpture to the creamy whiteness of the Noguchi lanterns. The folding screen is covered with tapestry in medieval motifs. Both rooms are architecturally the same —*treillage*. Both have palm trees, crystal chandelier, and zebra skin rugs. But the character of the two rooms is entirely different because of the furnishings.

2/all about beams

I have used beams for architectural interest in many, many rooms. I have used them in traditional rooms, in country rooms, in contemporary rooms. I love the effect of structural strength they give. And the beams are fake—that is, they are not solid wood. They are constructed of raw lumber and are hollow. People are constantly questioning me about them. If you share my enthusiasm for beams and have hesitated to use them in your own rooms because you thought they would require structural changes, hesitate no longer. I'll tell you how to do it.

First of all consider the size of your room and the effect that beams will give. I have a theory on the positioning of beams. If you're going to go to the trouble of doing them, you should have enough to make the effort worthwhile and the effect truly dramatic. As a general rule, I do not like to see ceiling beams placed any farther apart than two feet—that is, two feet of space between beams. Normally, for the average house that is not grand in scale a 6"×6" beam is an appropriate size to use. Anything smaller than this in even the smallest room is skimpy. Sometimes when a room is grand in scale you may need to go larger than that. Then I would still keep the width to six or eight inches, and change the depth of the beam (distance from the ceiling) to perhaps eight or ten inches—but the room would have to be fairly large.

In most instances it is best when installing

beams to put a border of wood all around the room at the ceiling. Standard lumber is normally three-quarters to seven-eighths inch thick. If you used wood of this normal thickness it wouldn't *look* strong enough to support the beams properly—even though they're hollow. Two pieces of lumber should be mitered together to give the illusion of lumber two inches thick. The depth measurement should be seven inches so that it is one inch deeper than your 6"×6" beams.

The baseboard, once again, can be made as simply as the border around the top, appearing to be two inches thick and either six inches or eight inches high, depending on the height of the room.

About lumber: Beams, baseboards and ceiling border should be made out of ordinary rough-sawn #2 pine or cedar. I like to use rough-sawn #2 grade because its imperfections and knotholes are more attractive. Number 2 is just as it comes from the sawmill before it is put through the sander. The saw blades catch in the grain of the wood and leave the waterfall graining in relief, which gives the wood a wonderful texture.

Constructing beams is a relatively simple thing for a carpenter or a do-it-yourselfer who has some feeling for old things.

After measuring the cross-room dimensions of your ceiling, assemble the beams with three pieces of lumber to form a hollow U shape.

Do not nail the bottom board to the side ones. The wood should be mitered and then the edges slightly broken with an axe or adze. Don't take chunks out of the wood, just "distress" the edges enough to take away the clean, sharp edges of the miter.

The beams can now be easily installed. Attach a block the size of the interior measure-ment of the hollow beam against the ceiling border on the wall at either end of the beam and toenail the beam into it. That's enough to hold it in place. You don't need additional support in the ceiling.

Finishing the Wood

Staining rough, rustic wood does not do the job. I have developed a formula for finishing beams, border and baseboards that gives a look so natural as to rival the real thing.

1. Apply a coat of rich ochre color casein paint. Casein is a water paint and dries very quickly.

2. Over the paint apply a coat of *clear* Butcher's Wax, paste formula, with an old paintbrush. (Let me stress, *only* Butcher's Wax. It's a brand name and available almost everywhere good paint and hardware are sold. Nothing else that I have tried seems to work as well as Butcher's Wax.)

3. After the first coat of wax has thoroughly dried, apply a second coat of *dark* (deep, rich brown) Butcher's Wax and allow this to dry. Then buff with as much energy as you have. This gives shining highlights to the wax.

4. If you are meticulous when it comes to detail you can use Japan Black (a black powder that you mix with water, also available in most paint stores) to put touches of dark shadows around the knotholes. You can also judiciously touch in streaks in the pattern of the grain where there would normally be sap streaks. Then soften the paint with a damp sponge. The final effect will be as real as you could possibly get without using old, distressed beams.

In Japan I visited a converted country farm-house—rare in the spate of modern construction going on today. While there I sketched the architectural details and reproduced them in this model room. Instead of squared-off beams whole logs are used in their natural state. The big support beam is a large tree, the smaller beams are smaller trees—the smallest are mere saplings. The walls are made of plaster mixed with straw, and while it doesn't show clearly in this photograph, the walls are actually "hairy."

The inspiration for this room came from an old Elizabethan manor house called Speke Hall. I used decorator's license and adapted the exterior treatment of Speke Hall for the inside of this room. The spaces in between the beams are filled with an off-white rough plaster. The lumber for the wall timbers and beams is rough sawn and distressed. The whole feeling of the room is seventeenth-century English cottage—with a touch of William and Mary in the desk. I particularly like the authentic elkhorn chair.

27

Here are many of my favorite architectural treatments in one room. The beams are used traditionally, but instead of being darkened and distressed, they're of natural rough-sawn cedar—grain, texture and knots all showing. The space between the beams that would be of rough plaster in a French country house is here covered with plexiglass and lit from behind for an up-to-date treatment. The banister of the stairway is a solid curved form in rough plaster. I particularly like the texture interplay between the rough wood, the sleek plexiglass and the rough plaster. The floor is covered in cocoa matting (the material used on diving boards), which adds still another texture. I combined country furniture with mirror chrome pedestals that contain hidden storage space behind concealed doors. The tops of the pedestals are illuminated to give uplight. The cupboard bed is a true copy of a bed design found in an old French book. It has a painted *faux bois* finish, but it could be any color. The accessories are a collection of Indian temple masks and baskets.

Beams need not be overwhelming. This ceiling would have been very plain, but the beams pull the vertical elements of the room together. I've broken one of my own rules by using different wall treatments in the same room— rough plaster, brick and wallpaper. Because of the beamed ceiling, the look is cohesive. The bookcase at the right of the photo is actually three-sided; it not only holds books but also acts as an architectural element to divide the room.

I got the idea for this room when I visited a Portuguese fisherman's cottage. Everything is quite typical here: The rough plaster, the rustic furniture, the rough-sawn blocks of blue painted wood on the floor, even the straw draped over poles suspended from the beams.

3/baseboards and moldings

They belong in a traditional room. They don't have to be dark and dowdy. They shouldn't be thought of as old hat.

Baseboards and stock cornice moldings are very important elements of the interior architecture for anyone whose decorating taste leans to the traditional. I think of moldings like a hat on a man. Moldings form a line between the wall and the ceiling and serve as a stop to the eye. Here's an opportunity to use color and line in decorating by painting the molding the same color as the walls (or a tone in the wallpaper) or a contrasting color for accent.

Baseboards and stock cornice moldings are usually taken for granted in rooms where they exist and not even thought about or budgeted for when absent. But these touches of interior architecture can lend interest to an otherwise plain apartment or house.

This is an extraordinary example of the use of moldings. The inspiration for this room is a library that I visited at the University of Coimbra in northern Portugal. There is a secret in the pilasters. They contain pull-out ladders, which can be braced with retractable iron rods to give access to the books on the top shelves. Extraordinary as the effect is, these are all stock moldings. They're simply combined in accordance with traditional shapes and with an eye to proportion. The moldings are then painted with casein paint and waxed coat after coat. The look is very elegant, but the ingredients are out of a lumber yard.

This basically seventeenth-century room is the result of considerable research. The molding around the top, with castles, lions and rosettes made of plaster, is definitely not stock, and must be made from plaster casts. But a simpler molding could be substituted. The general feeling of architectural strength comes from all the moldings, including those around the window and on the fireplace mantel. The walls are completely covered with tapestry, which is also used for the upholstery. The furniture matches the architectural details, being typically seventeenth century. I would call your attention to the simplicity of the accessories: Three wooden Indian temple figures on the cocktail table, and one enormous pewter charger to serve as an ashtray or just as decoration.

A Moorish feeling has been achieved here by the use of moldings, columns and pierced fretwork. The thick brackets supporting the soffit were made by gluing together many layers of wood which had been cut in the shape of the bracket. They are rather crude in feeling because this is an informal sitting room, but the design was authentic and came from a book on Moorish architecture.

This room is a box. The walls and ceiling are lacquered very heavily to give a finish as fine as an automobile's. But I framed the windows with a very authoritative molding; the shutters have been given a *faux marbre* finish to blend with the real marble on the floor.

A somewhat different use of moldings, and quite a simple one: Important crown molding and heavy base molding in a light finish that blends with the major furniture color in the room.

4/how to give a fireplace a facelift

Most of my inspiration for French, English and Italian mantels has come from the library, where I have searched out old books with either detailed drawings or photos of authentic fireplaces. They weren't just dreamed up in my mind. I may alter the size for proper scale, but the basic designs are authentic. There is lots of reference material available about fireplace construction—from the rough plaster forms of the southern coast of France and the Italian or Spanish coasts to the most traditional formal types. As elaborate as these designs might seem, duplicating them isn't that difficult. The important elements in a fireplace are the firebox and the flue. Everything else is superstructure, and once you've done a drawing that is properly scaled, the actual construction is not that complicated.

It's my observation that most fireplaces are awkwardly proportioned and badly scaled for the rooms they occupy. However, it's comparatively easy to improve their looks if the fireplace has reasonably good proportions.

Most important is the firebox—the place where the actual fire burns—which is usually surrounded by some kind of fire block or brick. Hopefully, it's brick or slate because they are the most attractive materials for fireplaces. If the firebox is good there are two ways to improve the looks of the fireplace:

1. A new chimney breast of plywood built from floor to ceiling can be given a handsome marble or wooden bolection molding. This is the typical molding used around fireplace openings. It's beautifully curved and heavy and simple to apply.

If the brick facing of the fireplace is sufficiently attractive you can band it with heavy, flat stainless steel molding about seven inches wide and one and one-half inches thick. This contrasts nicely with the brick for a contemporary look. You can also use marble molding.

2. You might leave your fireplace just as it is, provided there are not too many rows of brick above the opening, and add a new mantel. I like it when there is a seven- to nine-inch border of brick going around the actual opening—unless the fireplace is a major architectural feature, like a fireplace wall. Sometimes you'll see rows of brick over the fireplace opening as much as fifteen inches high, which is all out of proportion. Where you can, it would be good to remove the top layer of bricks till you get down to a reasonably even border around three sides of the firebox. Then there is a variety of period mantels that can be applied around the firebox, leaving a collar of brick exposed, which can either be left as it is or faced with slate or marble—depending on the formality or informality of the room. The wall above the mantel can then be mirrored, wallpapered or painted.

This is a fine example of a molded fireplace. The flue goes up into the ceiling and the fireplace is hung from it. There is space between the flue and the wall. I like its massive shape and the ledge that's built into the fireplace.

I brought this beautiful terra cotta mantel from Italy. It was made on a hillside overlooking Florence in a factory owned by the great-great-great grandsons of the founders. They still use the same methods for making terra cotta that were used when the factory was started. This is a typical example of a mantel that can be installed to surround an existing firebox completely. I am very pleased by the burnished antique finish that complements the warmth of the colors in the rest of the room.

This is a copy of an Early American mantel. I was taken by the folding doors with sturdy iron hardware that work like shutters to close off the fireplace completely. I believe this was done to keep out drafts when the fireplace wasn't in use. Probably the original chimney didn't have a damper. This is a typical Early American keeping room done in traditional colors.

In contrast to a heavily sculpted fireplace, this is a very uncomplicated round cylinder that is suspended from the ceiling over a brick hearth. You couldn't get simpler—or more modern.

The superstructure around this fireplace is more than is actually needed, but it does give the room a big, blocky look. The details I like best are the many levels that provide nooks and crannies for accessories. A note in passing: All the metal furniture in this room is copper, and the brown carpeting has inlaid copper strips. The rest of the room, including the fireplace superstructure, is dark brown.

This Empire mantel is much more formal than the type I usually choose. It is placed against a chimney breast built out about ten inches, with marble facing between it and the firebox.

Traditional bolection molding surrounds this firebox. The mantel has been built of stock moldings, painted to go with the wood trim of the room. The important superstructure is set against a built-out chimney breast and surrounded by antique mirror.

43

The details here are faithfully copied from authentic designs carefully researched. But the mantel has been constructed entirely of stock moldings and painted in *faux marbre*.

You would find this kind of mantel in a provincial house in the south of France. It's traditional Louis XV, and typically surrounds a large fireplace opening that is used for cooking.

The fireplace of this Spanish colonial room is built off the floor on a brick ledge. The mantel is finished in distressed wood to match the wood trim and beams in the room.

Nothing could be simpler or less fussy than
this bolection molding in black marble with
just the slightest graining of white.

The very grandeur of this room will give you some hint that it was based on a room in the Palazzo Davanzati in Florence. It embodies a little bit of almost everything we have talked about in architectural changes. Everything about it is authentic, from the design of the furniture to all of the architectural details. The beams are very real, the fireplace is an exact replica (although scaled down) of the original in the museum. In the original the walls were fresco, but I measured the elements of the design, rescaled them to fit this smaller room, and then had an artist paint them on canvas. The frieze around the ceiling and the baseboard are all *trompe l'oeil* to look like stone moldings. We faithfully reproduced the colors you would find in frescos that have been on the walls for many, many years—soft, muted. The windows are scaled-down replicas of those in the Palazzo Davanzati with very heavy, rough-sawn shutters studded with nail heads. That huge bellows is an exact replica, too. The furniture, with the exception of the sofa, is all seventeenth century and has been meticulously copied from the originals.

5/a touch of wood paneling

Wood paneling is still one of the most charming backgrounds for an intimate traditional room. Although it could never be considered inexpensive or simple, don't completely rule it out. If you're able to limit your paneling to straight lines and ninety-degree angles, half your problem is solved. Stock moldings can be used to create splendid effects.

The wall designs of seventeenth-century Spain, Italy, England and France had rectangular paneling and moldings. This wall treatment makes an excellent background for either the monastic look of seventeenth-century furniture so popular today or it can be an effective foil for important contemporary groupings. The curving lines and carving associated with both Regence and Louis XV boiserie are very beautiful, but they need to be produced by a hand carver or a fine cabinetmaker.

The moment you get into anything with a curved line it becomes much more expensive. However, if the curves are relatively simple it's possible to take a straight piece of molding and, if you have a very patient carpenter, he can put many, many saw cuts in the back of the molding, being careful not to cut all the way through (much like slicing French bread). The molding is then soaked in a bucket of water. When it's nailed into place in a curve and left to dry it stays curved. It's time consuming, but it's one way to achieve curved moldings without having them custom made.

For superb wood paneling in a clear, beautiful finish you need beautiful woods like walnut or cherry or one of the very precious woods. Highly sophisticated painted panels can be truly elegant, but they are costly because of the quality of workmanship and materials they require. If you want another traditional or country effect, try *my* version of painted wood paneling. Here the quality of the wood and the craftsmanship of construction are not so important—particularly if the final finish is to be distressed to achieve an antique appearance. My painted wood paneling requires the least expensive wood—like #2 pine, which comes with all kinds of irregularities like knotholes and rough saw marks. You can use boards cut to either standard or random widths and add suitable moldings. If the moldings are new and smooth you will have to distress them to match the rough finish of the wood. This is a great base for "antique" painting. Or the paneling can be whitewashed—the way I like it best—or painted any of a variety of colors.

One last note: Please don't construct ersatz panels by using rectangles of molding to break large flat areas of wall. Do a little research and do it like the experts. It's not easy, but it's not impossible.

Wood paneling is a very classic way to treat walls. This uses standard moldings painted in contrasting color, while the space between the moldings and the fields is marbled. This is a combination of paneled walls with an interesting beamed ceiling.

The walls in this lovely Regence paneled room would be extraordinarily costly if the paneling were real. This was all done in *trompe l'oeil*. The details were taken from a photograph of authentic Regence paneling but the walls are flat as can be, the paneling effect painted on. This is not the least expensive way to treat a wall, because the artist who does the painting must be unusually talented, but in the long run it would be not as expensive as real paneling in fine wood.

part II / from box to beautiful

6/fabric—
for soft walls

If you don't want elaborate construction details on your walls, try fabric. One way is to cover walls in shirred fabric, which gives them a lovely texture and lends great warmth to rooms. Because the entire effect depends on the use of yards and yards of fabric tightly shirred on rods between the crown molding and the baseboard, it makes sense to choose an inexpensive fabric. I recommend a modest cotton in either a solid color or small-scale overall pattern, a stripe or plaid. However, a highly glazed chintz can be very effective if you want a touch of shine on the walls.

Shirred fabric walls can take the place of elaborate architectural effects. But if you're using this technique remember that it's like painting. Wherever you would paint you have to have a panel of fabric—above and below windows, on a jog in the wall, everywhere. You can even have shirred walls in a heavily beamed room.

There are other ways to use fabric on walls. The most elaborate creates an effect that looks like upholstery. To start, tack laths at the ceiling line (or just below the cornice) and just above the baseboard. Add vertical strips every six feet. Then, between the lath strips, install either a heavy flannel or Dacron padding which will give the finished wall a soft, upholstered look. Stretch the fabric in all directions simultaneously and tack it to the laths, just as you would stretch canvas on a

frame for an oil painting. This lath-and-stretch method is very Old World and requires considerable skill.

Stapling fabric to walls is less expensive. It, too, requires great skill and can be professionally done. But if you feel up to the task, you can do it yourself.

1. Every piece of fabric has a woven edge called the selvedge. Measure the width of your fabric pattern only—do not measure the selvedge, which may be anything from one-quarter inch to one inch wide.

2. Start at a corner of the wall you're going to cover with fabric and mark off the exact width of your fabric. Then draw a vertical plumb line at that point from top to bottom. This is to assure putting the fabric on straight. Continue measuring and marking with plumb lines all across the wall. Now your wall will have a series of lines corresponding to the widths of your fabric.

3. Measure the distance of your wall from top (or molding) to bottom (top of baseboard) and cut a strip of fabric that length—plus three or four inches, for safety's sake.

4. Start at the right-hand corner of the room. Hold your strip of fabric (wrong side out) to the *right* of the corner, with the selvedge lapping over the corner to the left. This lap should be only the width of the selvedge. Using a staple gun, place staples evenly along the selvedge from top to bottom.

5. Cut strips of posterboard one and one-half inches wide. Place these strips over the already stapled selvedge of fabric, fitting the right-hand edge of the board as tightly as possible into the corner. Staple these strips from top to bottom.

6. Pull the fabric evenly from the corner to the left till it laps over the first plumb line to the left of the starting corner. If you have

measured correctly, the fabric will lap over the plumb line just the width of the selvedge. From top to bottom, place staples evenly on the selvedge to the *left* of the plumb line.

7. Take another strip of fabric and staple it wrong side out on the selvedge, directly over the previous strip of fabric. These staples, too, must be at the left of the plumb line.

8. Repeat the stapling of a posterboard strip from top to bottom on top of the double layer of selvedge so that the *right* edge of the strip is exactly over the plumb line. When the strip is attached, pull your fabric over the board toward the next plumb line on the left. You now have a very neat joining of the two panels of fabric.

Continue in this manner, repeating steps 6, 7 and 8. When you come to the end of the wall on the left it will be necessary to fold the selvedge under and staple it as closely into the corner as possible. Your staples will show, but you'll be covering them with trim.

When your wall is covered with fabric (either stapled, or using the European padding method) you'll want double welt, braid or nailheads to finish off the edges—particularly at the top and bottom of the fabric and around any openings. Depending on what kind of job you've done, you'll really need this trim around all edges to cover up raw ends or staples that show.

The draperies for a room with fabric-covered walls should be in the same fabric. When a room has this rich, fabric-y feeling, I like to upholster the main pieces of furniture in the same fabric as the walls. Smaller upholstered pieces can then serve as accents in color or pattern (see Part V, Living Color).

Another fabric for your walls could be bedspreads. There is a great variety of woven or printed bedspreads that come from the Far East and India. They have marvelous, paisley-like designs in earth tones and combinations of blue, red and tan that are terribly effective. You'll find more and more of them appearing in the shops.

I like to use bordered bedspreads because the borders can give the effect of panels on the wall. This involves a little more work than straight fabric, because you have to measure your walls and bedspreads carefully to achieve symmetry and balance. Also, there is a certain amount of waste, but the bedspreads I'm talking about are so inexpensive that you can afford a little waste.

Fabric can be applied to walls like wallpaper if you have the right kind of paste. But it's tricky to do and should be done by a professional. There are also paper-backed fabrics made for wall application. However, they really look like wallpaper and if you're going to put fabric on a wall, why not get the effect of softness? Even when you don't use padding under the fabric, it hangs on the wall softly and gives a true *fabric* look.

The walls in this room are completely upholstered in an ivory-colored silk rep which repeats the color of the silk on the sofa and picks up the color in the Coromandel screen. It forms a very subtle, soft background for the formal living room furniture. In the dining room beyond you'll see the same fabric printed in a damask pattern. The pattern is the same red as that in the screen and the accent colors in the living room. The printed dining room fabric is then used for the draped table at the end of the sofa.

The mood of this room is very museum-y, deliberately so. It was a re-creation of a room I had seen in a palace in Portugal. The walls are all upholstered in strips of golden silk. The crown moldings and baseboards are exceptionally beautiful. Then, separating the panels of fabric and flanking the baseboard and crown molding is a luxurious trimming, which is repeated on the bedspread and on the draperies. The floor is carefully laid plywood painted in many colors to look like marble:

In the seventeenth century it was not unusual to have walls covered with painted or tooled leather. Here, I have simulated this treatment with a heavy, leather-textured vinyl, the "texture" applied by an artist in a typical seventeenth-century design. The effect is very mellow, as well as unusual.

Broken rules again—using two different materials on walls. On the left-hand wall, cognac antique velvet from floor to ceiling, and adjacent to it, a wall of polished aluminum. The disparity of materials gives the aluminum-covered wall an architectural feeling, a nice contrast with the softness of the velvet pile. Against all this, traditional Spanish pine furniture in a very mellow finish, and, mixed with it, very modern, boxlike teak cases with stainless steel hardware.

The walls of this room have been upholstered in lightweight raw silk in a natural shade. The variations in the texture of the silk provide a soft background for a traditional room and a warm contrast to the stainless steel furniture.

Another of my favorite wall treatments: Draped walls. The fabric is shirred all around the room on rods just below the ceiling. The étagères are spaced so that all the books show when the draperies are caught back. The draperies can also be released from their tiebacks to create a completely draped wall. The fabric is lightweight China silk in a gray taupe and is trimmed in chamois-colored velvet ribbon which matches the chamois-colored suede on the sofa.

Here, the inexpensive printed cotton Indian bedspreads I have mentioned are used as wall covering. I cut up the bedspreads to form paneling on the wall and then incorporated the border of the bedspreads into the valances for the draperies. Even the sofa and chair are covered in the same bedspread fabric.

This is an unusual wall treatment for a little boy's room. There is a museum in the town of Epinal in southern France that has all kinds of historic engravings of French life. I had blowups of some of these engravings made on canvas—they all have military themes—and applied them to the wall. It not only makes an interesting wall treatment for a boy's room, but injects a little art and history into the atmosphere.

Striped velvet in a gray taupe color gives a softly linear effect as a background for a library-sitting room.

In this man's sitting room the walls are covered in leather from floor to ceiling—really rugged cowhide with the brand marks and scars still visible. The leather was left in its natural color with a coat of wax applied for protection. There's another strong masculine note in the campaign furniture and the stainless steel étagères and chair frames. The Oriental rug pulls together the colors of the leather and adds a warm touch of red.

You have a room that could serve as a library and you want to go far out. Here's a way to do it. The basic moldings are stock, but the friezes are painted by an artist. The walls are covered with replicas of Pompeiian frescos painted on wooden panels, which were then antiqued and waxed. The pilasters around the windows are painted to look like malachite. This would also make a dramatic foyer. Or a bathroom that would be very grand, indeed.

This room would certainly belong to a member of the Saturday Generation. The walls, ceiling and floor were all painted white. And then supergraphics were stenciled on the walls as were the circles on the floor . . . both over the basic white paint job.

This room was an absolute box. No moldings, no trim, no adornment. But the walls,
ceiling and floor were painted a vibrant red.
Then I designed a supergraphic to run across
the floor, up the wall, over the ceiling and
back down again. If you have a steady hand
and are totally liberated in your love of
color, even with a minimum of furniture, you
can make a dramatic statement like this.

7/and then there's paint

Volumes have been written on the subject: The colors you select for your walls can do wonders for changing the apparent size of a room. While it is technically true that light colors and grayed tones do make a room look larger, and that warm, advancing colors such as terra cotta, brown and deep gray seem to decrease its apparent size, personally I don't care. I have a different philosophy.

As far as I'm concerned, only a wall of mirror really makes a room look larger. It also lends brightness. Your room is small? All right, the paint color isn't going to make it any larger. It only makes it look a *little* larger. If you have a small room and you love deep-toned, rich colors, use them and dramatize the room. Yes, it's small, but it's gorgeous, charming and intimate. But it *is* important to keep everything in the room in tones of the same color to hold things together.

And if you're decorating a large room and want it to look smaller, painting it with dark colors won't do much to achieve that illusion for you. The trick is to bring furniture arrangements into the center of the room to minimize the open spaces. More of this in Chapter 11 on room planning. The moral is: Paint your walls the color you want regardless of the rules. One exception is a very dark room, without natural light, in which you've got to achieve a light, airy feeling to avoid claustrophobia.

In nearly every instance, paint or paper all walls in a room in the same paint or paper. I dislike two elements in one room unless there is a strong architectural reason for such a combination. This whole business of having the two end walls done in a different color in order to distract from the narrowness of a room is highly suspect. I'm not contending that it doesn't make the room look less long and narrow. But the decorating effect achieved in the end is so terrible, in my mind, that it just isn't worth it.

I'd rather accept the fact that I've got a long room and cut the length with a desk or work-table coming out from the wall. It's the greatest decorating trick I know, and I have used it many, many times.

About woodwork: If it isn't attractive, paint it the color of the walls. If it is attractive, if you have beautifully contoured crown moldings and baseboards, then put the woodwork to work for you. There are many cases where woodwork can be in a contrasting accent color or lacquered or marbled.

Woodwork can be painted the same color as the walls but striped in an accent color (striped very lightly and rubbed off before the paint dries) to give a broken ribbon effect. But don't paint just one stripe on crown molding. Use at least two or three, even though one is a hairline. Never use just one big band of brightness on woodwork—crown moldings or baseboards.

One final note on wall color: Get a big sample of the color to approve. People come to me with thumbnail-size chips asking if the color is right. I can never tell—even with all my years of experience in specifying color. I always use a 5" x 7" or 8" x 10" color sample that the painters prepare for me. I put it up on a wall of the room that's to be painted to see how it looks in the light that will fall on it—

incandescent or fluorescent or a combination of both. Light changes the attitude of a color. This is especially true in your home. Put up a sample of paint and look at it in the morning, the afternoon, the evening, when lamps are all lit. Be sure you have a color that works well throughout the day and evening. Even if a color passes all these tests, it's generally much better in one kind of light. So you should determine the color that looks best when you use the room most.

Notes on Wallpaper

Wallpaper is probably the least expensive way to dramatize a room that's devoid of any architectural interest. I love wallpaper in an entrance hall, a bedroom, a kitchen, but usually not in the room where you spend a lot of time. I could, on the other hand, contradict that. I can think of special situations where wallpaper in very soft or muted tones (and I don't mean dull or drab) forms a suitable background for a much-used area.

Wallpaper can be very gratifying in the dining room—a room used for short periods where the lighting, I would assume, is fairly low. Candlelight is my preference. In low light you see just a glimmer of pattern on the wall—a peripheral aura in the room.

But, please, buy good wallpaper. I mean well-drawn, well-colored, beautifully scaled wallpaper. Much that's available is hideous. Splendid, well-colored wallpaper can be a tremendous help to a room.

Scale is something else to consider. I love large-scale wallpaper in a foyer as long as the color and pattern don't annihilate what's going on in rooms adjacent to the foyer.

8/how to treat a window

Windows come in all sizes and shapes. Some of the most beautiful are French doors. I love the look of them, the way they go right down to the floor. The proportion is lovely—without that sudden stop at a window sill. Just as beautiful are big bay windows or large traditional picture windows with lots of panes to give a heavily mullioned look and always with hefty, dramatic molding to frame them.

French doors are relatively rare in today's building, and it's not always possible to install them in a house or apartment. But if you're planning any renovation or you're in the process of building a house, I can enthusiastically recommend either French doors or tall traditional windows for the drama (to say nothing of the light) they lend a room.

Regardless of the shape or size of windows, there are ways of treating them to blend with any style of decoration. Without doubt, the look I favor for traditional rooms is tieback draperies with a valance framing the top. This suits windows three to five feet wide. By the way, there are no such things as drapes. "Drape" is a verb. The fabric surrounding a window is called draperies or a drapery treatment.

If you're not using draperies, then I like a more architectural treatment, with windows that are shuttered and have an interesting molding surrounding them. You can choose either louvered shutters or crisscross lattice work to create the look of doors. This treatment allows you to see through the windows yet provides window dressing that relieves a naked look.

When selecting color and fabric for a drapery treatment, you have only three decisions to make to be certain that the draperies harmonize with the room. They should be either the same color as the wall or the same color as the major upholstery (in either the same fabric or in a different texture of the same color) or they can be in the accent color of the room. I go into more detail about this in Part V on Living Color.

Texture and color are the most important considerations in the selection of fabric. I lean toward woolens, linens, heavy cottons, Siamese silk and fabrics that are generally rich in color. I mention these fabrics particularly (and use them over and over again) because of the vibrancy of their color—because they articulate color so brilliantly. There is nothing like wool to hold the color of dye. The same is true of linen and cotton—any of the natural fibers. And Siamese silk! Even if you're choosing a neutral color, there is a great richness to it. These are my favorites, although there are many other fabrics available which would be suitable for draperies.

I have a pet *dislike* when it comes to drapery treatments: Passé, unabashed camouflage treatments called wall-to-wall. They overburden a room with fabric. Furthermore, nine out of ten times, if there are wall-to-wall draperies the person responsible for them got carried away and used either an abstract pattern or some big splashy design that overwhelms the room. The only time I like pattern in draperies is when it forms an integral part of the decoration of a room. If you have a small or narrow window, drape it and say, "Okay, my window is narrow. Here it is."

Don't cover every inch of wall around it. A window is particularly attractive if it is surrounded by wall space that frames it like matting around a picture.

It's very sad to see fabric in window treatments that is skimpy—whether it's sheer, unlined curtains or draperies. Fabric at windows needs lots and lots of fullness. For sheer curtains the fabric should be three times the width of the window—really voluptuous and full, with deep, double 10-inch hems, not little, skimpy shirttail hems at the bottoms. Draperies, too, should be lush and full.

Curtains should be made in a plain, unlined fabric with an interesting texture that will show as the light shines through the fabric; draperies should be lined as well as interlined. The lining not only makes them hang better and accents their full, lush folds, but it protects the fabric against the sun and prevents light from shining through and disfiguring the fabric.

I have very few rules about draperies, but there is one: In almost every instance the draperies should be full length unless there is a radiator enclosure built out at window sill level making floor length impossible. That's about the only reason I can think of for having short draperies, which cut the look of a window in half and spoil the design of a room. When I say floor length I mean they just should be touching the floor, not two inches above the floor, not draping all over the floor. That's an elegant, overstated look, but it belongs to another era.

Finishing draperies at the top is simple. There are two possibilities:

1. A buckram valance (which I prefer) with either a straight edge (if it's a small window) or a shaped valance. It depends on the design of the room. A shaped valance can be either

a scalloped edge or some kind of geometric form. Just like the crown moldings in the architecture of a room, a valance is like a hat on a man. It becomes an architectural element that holds the room together. A proper size valance for a nine-foot window would be approximately twelve inches deep.

Most of the time I like to see a ribbon trim or some kind of braid finishing off the center and bottom edges of the draperies, and also trimming the tiebacks and valance.

2. If you choose not to use a valance, you can use wooden, brass or fabric-covered poles with rings as an attractive way to support the draperies.

Draperies can be used in combination with shuttered windows, bamboo or tortoise-shell blinds, simple, lightweight sheer curtains or Roman shades.

Roman shades are flat, fabric panels that operate like window shades. They rise in a straight line, gathering in horizontal folds as they do so. They're very tailored and neat and work well when used alone for a more contemporary treatment or—in more elaborate rooms—used in combination with draperies. They can be placed on either narrow or wide windows. They are very effective in single units, but as they get wider they're more attractive if they have vertical bands of fabric or trimming sewed on them to break up the expanse of fabric. Roman shades can be in solid colors or prints, but I prefer them in solid colors banded by a contrasting color. The bands also serve to conceal the stitching, where the cords are run up the back, and can be used to pick up an accent color in a room.

So far, we have talked mostly about window treatments for traditional rooms, but there are treatments that will lend interest to modern rooms as well.

I have an aversion to large, contemporary windows that are draped in yards and yards of fabric, which has to be pulled back when more light is wanted. I have seen some windows designed with pockets in the walls at their sides so that when the curtains are pulled back they almost disappear in architectural recesses. But most contemporary window treatments leave you with great bunches of fabric in the corners of the room. Not very pretty.

In a contemporary room I love the look of very narrow metal Venetian blinds with slats about one inch wide. They come in every color of the rainbow, and in polished and brushed chrome. They not only filter light but give some adornment to the window. I also like vertical blinds. They're very successful in a contemporary room, but only in white (or off-white), polished chrome or brushed steel. Vertical blinds have a certain crispness that demands that they be respected as an architectural element. If they're chrome, they're very exciting when partially opened, giving a mirror reflection as well as admitting light through the slats.

Other window treatments I have used are pierced wood Indian screens for a traditional look and, borrowing from the Japanese shoji screen, smoked or white translucent plexiglass in simple frames set on slides that can be completely pushed aside for openness or shut for privacy and light control. Sliding screens of this kind can also be set with metal grillwork in a very simple design.

Valances and Tieback Draperies

Valances as architecture unify a room through dramatic design that contrasts with the simplicity of draperies, walls and bed hangings—all in the same color of linen.

Valances springing from the wall and ceiling fabric to form a structural separation between rooms demonstrate a window treatment used as architecture. The same treatment is used on windows at the opposite side of the room.

A softer, more feminine look is achieved by bouffant draperies in bleached white linen with a perky valance and edging of accordian-pleated ruffles. The contrasting ribbon trim acts as a frame for the draperies and echoes the architectural details.

A simple treatment to blend with straight-line contemporary furniture, these draperies and valances have a double banding in ribbon trim to accent the angular shape of room elements.

To Drape or Not to Drape

Windows with a strong Persian influence: Hinged wooden fretwork doors separated by twisted columns give these windows architectural impact.

A wall of painted shutters, Bermuda style, opening out to catch the tropical breeze. Drama without drapery.

Two adaptations of the Japanese shoji, one in translucent natural linen stretched in window frames, which continues the natural raw silk look of the walls, the other in a pristine white setting is a damask pattern printed in white on sheer white batiste. If you look closely, you'll see that these two photos are of the same room with architectural changes. They were done one year apart at Bloomingdale's.

Wood as Drapery

In a more rustic setting, a heavily but traditionally pine-shuttered window needs no fabric. I bought this entire window in Madrid, brought it back and designed a whole room around it.

If the moldings are strong enough and the shutters are bold enough and they're painted to blend with the room, no fabric is called for —especially next to the strength of the wallpaper pattern.

A small window on a balcony simply treated by using traditional French balloon toile for a valance that repeats the shape of the wood trim and finishing it off with trim little tieback draperies.

A lambrequin is a valance that goes all around three sides of a window. There are many ways it can be used to frame a window. Here, the simplicity of the shape makes it, in the Japanese tradition, *shibui*.

Draperies on wooden poles and hung on wooden rings serve as both window treatment and room division. Here, in the same printed linen as the wall covering, they unify the room.

The lambrequin as a wall extension, covered in the same bleached linen as the wall covering, relates to the room architecture more than the window treatment fabric—in this case, bleached white batiste in a recessed and shuttered window.

Beads. Use them carefully. Here, they're a room divider leading to a sleeping nook. The glitter of crystal is toned down by a border design that suggests fabric. The total effect is compelling and makes curtains and draperies unnecessary on the window beyond.

Have a little fun with a valance and add room dimension like this. It's a great way to handle an arch-top window. It could as easily have been done with a flat valance following the contour of the arch—but this is more diverting.

9/pitch a tent

Tents are a startling way to dramatize an area that might otherwise be lackluster. They're a way to hide bad architecture, too, because when you tent a room you are visually constructing it in hung fabric. I would never lead you to believe that tents are simple. They're not. And they're nigh on to impossible to do without professional help. But they are striking.

When using a patterned fabric for a tent, I like to use stripes. With such large masses of patterned fabric, stripes work well because they can be mitered at the corners, working in from the walls to the center to form concentric squares.

With a tent you ordinarily need a valance around the room. Here again, stripes are versatile and make any valance crisp and interesting.

Tents can be made of almost any fabric from the most elaborate fabric to the most inexpensive (and I would advise an inexpensive fabric because of the miles of yardage needed).

I feel that the ceiling and walls should be done in matching fabric. A tent is not a tent with only a draped ceiling. And the entrance to the room should have tieback draperies so that you have a real tent feeling when you enter the room. The ceiling of a tent should fall in soft folds and look unconstructed. One way to get this soft look is to attach the fabric at the edges of the ceiling and at the very center and let the fabric dip between the points of attachment at center and sides.

A tent treatment works well for any room in the house. Tented foyers can be delightful. Long hallways leading to other rooms in the house can be tented, as can dining rooms and bedrooms. Unless you're of a very exotic persuasion, a tented living room is a little far out.

This is a tented bath-dressing room for a man. The fabric is a printed, textured linen. The classic design of the print dictated the shape of the valance.

Tents can be beautifully simple and elegant or very exotic, depending on the fabric used. You can choose almost any kind of fabric imaginable, from a tiny little stripe to a small, allover pattern, to natural canvas with leather trim. The Pakistani tent shown here is a good example of the exotic.

part III/underfoot

10/bare and bedecked

To be basic, when it comes to finishing floors in a room you have three choices: Bare, partly covered with area rugs, carpeted.

Because I happen to like highly polished floors, let's start with those. Whether it's a fine and fabulous floor of hardwood, or waxed terra cotta quarry tiles, glazed ceramic tiles or shiny vinyl, the glimmer and glow that a polish lends can be a decorative dimension in a room. The luster of a polished floor gives a rich, reflective quality. When you look at a table placed on a polished floor, you not only see the table, you see a reflection of its form on the floor. This is true in broad daylight as well as in artificial night light.

But let's go to the opposite extreme. One room that I did was divided into three levels: A living or conversation pit area, a dining and a work area. I carpeted *every inch* of the room —the ceiling, walls, floor, sides of the seating pit—everything was carpeted in the same color of deep gray in a very durable industrial quality carpeting. It resembled nothing so much as the look of thick felt. This particular type of carpeting came with and without a rubber backing. I put the rubber-backed carpet on all the floor and pit areas and the un-backed carpet on the walls. This created a warm, cavelike atmosphere, enhanced further by very dark upholstery in wool tweed, the same dark gray that exactly matched the color of the carpet. This consistency of texture and color created the ultimate in unity of feeling. An overall upholstered look can be achieved in any of the lighter, brighter colors, too. Particularly when there are ledges that are used for additional seating space. In carpeting everything you get a very luxurious feeling. More and more I feel this is an interesting direction to take in room decoration. It's not done very much, and it has a great range of possibilities.

From total carpeting, we advance to complete floor carpeting—usually called wall-to-wall. I love total carpet in a bedroom—everything from very shaggy to flat, hard pile.

It's a great comfort to step out of bed onto a warmly carpeted floor.

But I have used carpeting in other rooms, too. In some cases I have divided the carpeted area with lineal strips of stainless steel or polished chrome to form concentric squares or stripes. The carpeted spaces between metal strips were about thirty inches, the strips one-inch to one and one-half inches wide, and as thick as the carpeting so that they didn't form ridges. Certainly, there are times when a room calls for a broad expanse of carpeting, and I find it pleasing to the eye to break up the flat area with architectural strips.

Area Rugs

Area rugs are important. They can draw a section of the room together in a cohesive unit, but care must be exercised that area rugs be of the right size, color and design.

I like the look of area rugs working with the major upholstered furniture group, holding it together like a raft. At the top of my list is square rugs. For instance, if you have a seven- or eight-foot sofa, I prefer an eight-foot square rug forming the boundary for the seating group, with most of the furniture sitting *off* the rug. On the rug would be a cocktail table and maybe an occasional chair on the opposite side from the sofa and facing into the grouping diagonally.

Area rugs can be smooth and velvety or they can be long-haired and shaggy. They can be an allover pattern, or they can be one color with another shade as a border, depending on the amount of pattern in the room. When it comes to country settings, I lean toward shaggy rugs. With seventeenth-century furniture I like Oriental rugs and heavily patterned rugs in the traditional native styles of India or Morocco.

Here's a fine example of a country Indian rug. The natural colors in it form a beautiful accent to an otherwise all-white room. Color accents in the room spring from the colors in the rug—the mattress on the bed and in the matting of the miniature Indian paintings grouped on the wall.

Here the rug forms an island of pattern and color in an otherwise sparse room.

In this very traditional guest bedroom, the area in front of the daybed is defined by an Indian chain-stitch rug in a delicate, allover hand-woven design. It has an antique look. This style of rug has been done for ages in India, but it is actually a contemporary reproduction. The patterns and colors repeat the accents in the room and unify the visual effect.

The very classic fretwork pattern is repeated in the elaborate details on the cornice molding and in the rug border. It's all a beautiful complement to the elaborate reproduction of the Pompeiian frescos. The rug, you'll note, is the same width as the sofa and forms a raft for the furniture group. Sometimes frescos or murals can give impact to a room—but only when beautifully painted.

Carpeted with Light

In this living room the entire floor was constructed of wooden grid set with white translucent squares of plexiglass. The room is all white and wallpapered in an industrial material with a steel metallic finish. The light used under the grid is fluorescent because it gives off less heat than incandescent lighting and needs less ventilation.

90

Vinyl and Tile

Here is an elegant dining room floored in black, shiny marbleized vinyl with insets. This is a very classic pattern, one that can be seen in real marble in European palaces. That's the ultimate in floor treatment. It can be done in this country, but the cost would be prohibitive. Vinyl is nearly as effective. Just as in carpeting, I like a border on an all-vinyl floor. It defines the shape of the room.

Contemporary-looking though it is, the design for this vinyl floor was taken from one of the old Dutch masters—Pieter de Hooch. Here, I switched elements and draped an Oriental rug over the table.

A solid white vinyl floor, the tiles of which have beveled edges. It's an important detail because it gives the floor a little texture and defines the pattern of the tiles that are sleek and shiny and all one color.

Regular octagonal-shaped quarry tiles in good old terra cotta color. This is the traditional color and pattern that has been used in houses all over the world. In Europe today you can see houses with the floors in all the major rooms done in terra cotta tiles. The patina that comes after years of waxing and polishing is something that simply cannot be matched for beauty.

Here is another shape tiles can take. These are a deep, rich brown, very irregularly mottled and with a fine, high glaze.

And here the ceramic tile is all white with a pebble-like finish.

One floor treatment not terribly expensive to do. Rough-sawn boards (the kind used for beams that we discussed in Chapter 2) are put down in either regular widths or random widths or, as here, in a herringbone pattern. The boards should be put down loosely—not tightly fitted together. As the boards age, dry and are walked on they tend to separate. The resulting irregular spaces between the boards look just as they would in an old house.

There is nothing like brick for floors—particularly in a country kitchen or in an old house. But it must be old brick—used brick—waxed to give a protective coating to save the floor from spills. As with terra cotta tiles, brick gives a natural look to a room.

You can paint floors, too, with casein paint in any color—orange, yellow, green, whatever you like. Then cover the floor with Butcher's Wax, buffed and buffed and buffed to a fine shine. I wouldn't recommend this floor treatment for a room that gets a lot of heavy foot traffic, for it wears thin after a while. But used judiciously, it's very effective.

Bare floors, tile floors, ceramic floors, area rugs or carpeting, you have a number of choices when it comes to floor treatment. As in any decorating, what you do with your floors will depend on what you're doing with the rest of the room. But don't just ignore floors. They must be as carefully thought out as wall treatments and furniture arrangement. After all, a floor is a lot more than just something that the furniture sits on.

part IV/choosing furniture

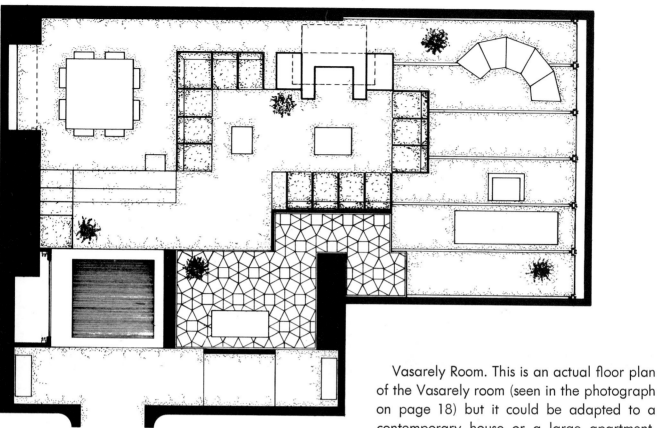

Vasarely Room. This is an actual floor plan of the Vasarely room (seen in the photograph on page 18) but it could be adapted to a contemporary house or a large apartment. The plan is multilevel—seven in all. The entrance is at ground level, and entering the room you would step up two levels to a floor set in stainless steel tiles (indicated by the triangled area). The main living area is all upholstered in gray carpeting. The fireplace opposite the entrance is free standing; the area behind it forms a corridor that leads from the work area to the dining area without having to descend into the conversation pit, which is at the lowest level in the room. Immediately opposite the entrance, the shaded area indicates a pool, which serves only as a divider between the entry and the living spaces. This is a room that typifies my theory of dividing rooms with "cubes in space," which is really what multi-level construction is for—space division without walls.

11/the important first step— a floor plan

I cannot stress enough the importance of a floor plan.

Whether you already have some pieces of furniture that you're going to keep and plan to buy others or you're going to buy a piece at a time, you should have an accurate floor plan. Not only of the room itself, but of the furniture arranged in it—even though you might not complete the plan for five years. You should have a proper anxiety about budget, too. Seriously consider the budget now and what you can hope to acquire in the future.

It may seem a little inflexible to have a floor plan and to lock yourself into it. But if you consider the design of a room, there are not a lot of possibilities for variations of arrangement. The average room has only one place (and a possible second) that is right for a sofa. Unless you are blessed with an enormous room, perfectly proportioned, and can have a sofa and conversation group in four or five different places, one floor plan will work for you.

I'm amazed at people who can stand in an empty room and say, "I'll put the sofa over there." That could be absolutely the wrong place to put the sofa. I can't figure out the arrangement of a room that way, and I'm a professional. Any professional will tell you that you can't design without a floor plan.

You might think of a floor plan for a room as you would a recipe for something you create in the kitchen. You don't go into the kitchen and ad lib the recipe of bouche à la reine. If your floor plan is well worked out, if it makes a good graphic design on paper, chances are the completed room will be beautifully balanced.

There are three steps to making a floor plan:

1. A room plan drawn to scale
2. Proper choice of furniture
3. A completed floor plan with furniture placed for best balance and design

Let's take up step 1.

The Room Plan

First, measure the room with either a steel tape measure or a folding wooden ruler. Don't use an ordinary cloth tape measure because it stretches and your measurements may not be accurate. Measure the length of walls, the places where doorways and windows occur, their measurements and the distances between them, and any architecural variations like a jog in the wall, a fireplace, a protruding radiator enclosure.

Then draw up your room plan, using a scale $1/4'' = 1'$. I find this scale the easiest to handle without taking up large sheets of paper.

Next, measure each of the walls the same way: Width, height, doorways, windows, the distance from the ceiling to floor, the measurements of any architectural features.

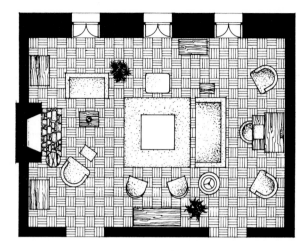

Living Room. This is a good example of a floor plan with furniture out in the center of the room. The fireplace on the short end of the room is faced by the sofa out in the center, breaking up the long line of the room. The height of the fireplace is balanced by a tall secretary, approximately the same height as the three pairs of French doors on the opposite side of the room.

Now we're ready for the decisions you'll have to make about placing furniture in this bare room plan. But before we approach that, a note:

Do-It-Yourself—Yes or No?

Although this book is all about decorating and written to be helpful, unless you are endowed with some talent and flair for decorating and have some experience express- ing it, I wouldn't advise your dashing out and starting to decorate. As a professional, I know what it takes in knowledge and experience to design well, and I have a well-founded respect for my fellow professionals.

The best service this book can offer you is to start you *thinking* about decorating, to tell you how decorating is done, to make you aware of color and form and balance and give you a feeling of period. Then, when it comes time to make important decisions (and important purchases) seek professional help. It will save you in the long run.

It is part of the service of the design depart- ment of any fine store to do complete plans and arrangements for you and be available for consultation. Even in the case of the floor plan you have worked out, a professional eye would probably be advisable before you plunge. Decorating is like meal planning. You plan what dishes you would like to serve, but when it comes to the actual cooking you will do best to follow a recipe worked out for you by a professional.

Now to the choice and arrangement of furniture.

12/choosing the proper furniture

I have discovered over the course of the years that the style of furniture selected for a room is much less important to the total effect of a room than are the color scheme and the furniture arrangement, the window treatment and accessories. The most beautiful pieces of furniture poorly placed and in a drab color scheme are lost. Let's face it, you can't just neglect a beautiful piece of furniture. It needs to be complemented. Let's go about it systematically. There are two kinds of furniture used in a room: Upholstered furniture and wooden furniture. Let's think about these for a moment.

Upholstered Furniture

When I speak of upholstered furniture I mean well-designed (repeat, well-designed) fully upholstered furniture. Sofas that are built to the ground just rising on small hidden casters or with simple skirts to the floor with no more adornment than pleats at the corner. Then there are love seats and completely upholstered chairs.

A banquette is a major upholstered piece. Banquettes can be quite traditional looking but are a somewhat more contemporary approach to the decoration of a traditional room. Banquettes come in many different styles. They can have skirts to the floor. Sometimes they are

very modern and sleek looking or they can be really quite soft with loose cushions. They come not only as individual armless chairs but in two-seaters and three-seaters without arms and in corner units so that they can all be joined together to make L-shaped, U-shaped, even square arrangements.

Modular seating units are also in the upholstered furniture class. Modular seating is composed of individual armless chairs that are generally very modern in concept. The individual base units have a cushion and a construction that permits plugging in arms. Some units are like a hassock with sockets for plugging in backs. You can use as many of these units as you want, joining them together to form zigzags, squares, conversation pits, almost limitless arrangements. Sometimes modular units can be used in a room to the complete exclusion of chairs or any other seating-type furniture.

Another piece of furniture that I consider important is the wing chair. Whenever I do a traditional room, I invariably use a wing chair. It's the one chair that has enough height and bulk to balance a sofa or a love seat (we're coming to the principles of balance in a moment).

Most other chairs are small in bulk and I generally prefer to use them in pairs. But a wing chair can sit by itself in a grouping. The wing chair has its counterpart in modern. It's called a big chair, and it should have a distinctive sculptural form which gives it enough bulk and importance to use opposite a sofa grouping and still maintain balance in the room.

Open arm chairs are the final class of upholstered furniture. Open arm chairs—also called occasional chairs—with upholstered seats and backs are an important element in designing a room, for, in addition to being comfortable, they don't take up too much room and they relieve a too-upholstered look. Also, they can be shifted easily if occasion demands because they are light in weight. Too, because they present a limited upholstered surface they can be used to introduce a brightly colored or patterned fabric which serves as an accent color in a room. (More of that in Part V.)

Open arm chairs can be any style that fits your room, ranging from Louis XIII (massive, heavily turned wood legs) to the more graceful Louis XV (peasant or quite formal) to the most modern steel and leather chairs designed by Mies van der Rohe or Breuer.

Wooden Furniture

In the simplest possible terms, wooden furniture is anything that is not upholstered. This would include desks or worktables, commodes, cocktail tables, lamp and tea tables, etc. Bigger wooden pieces would be armoires, library cabinets, bookshelves (and sometimes étagères) and console tables.

I find that a half-and-half mix of upholstered pieces and wooden pieces is ideal for most rooms. Over the course of years I've found that there aren't too many pieces of furniture that go into a living room. Usually, in addition to the upholstered seating pieces, there are a desk, a cocktail table, lamp tables and one important wooden piece like an armoire, a library cabinet, or a commode. That's about all that will go comfortably in a living room, so there aren't all that many decisions to make about the 50/50 mix between upholstered pieces and wooden pieces.

The Balance Points

Don't fall into the trap of putting most of the furniture around the perimeter of a room. It's easy, certainly, but it's dull. Good design in a room depends on having two balance points. The first is the major grouping of large upholstered pieces. They should be together for conversation, and their combined mass takes up a major area of the room.

The second balance point in a room can be architectural: A big, interesting fireplace, a major book wall, a big bay window with a wide expanse of glass. If there is no large mass architecturally and your room is more of a box, then you'll have to *create* another balance point to offset the massed upholstery and conversation pieces. So let's take up the first balance point.

The Conversation Pieces

One of my classic arrangements is this: Whenever I have a sofa, I invariably have a pair of chairs at right-angles to it, and opposite it another chair that stands alone. In a traditional room this "loner" chair is usually a wing chair. In a more contemporary room with a modern sofa, I might compose this basic group with a pair of steel-and-leather chairs and an odd chair in a big, distinctive, sculptural style. In a smaller room, my basic group might be a smaller sofa, a pair of upholstered chairs and one open arm chair.

Now, because every place to sit should have a table surface near it for light, for a place to put a drink, a book, an ashtray, within this basic conversation grouping of upholstered pieces go certain obvious wooden pieces: A large cocktail table (preferably square), lamp tables and such.

We now have the nucleus of the conversation group, but it's not enough. I believe in having something like a desk or worktable in every room. I particularly like a desk placed at right angles to a sofa and facing into the center of the conversation group. A desk requires a small chair, and the combination of the two at right angles to the sofa balances nicely with the pair of chairs at the opposite end of the sofa. When you think about it, a desk (or worktable) and an upholstered piece like a chair or sofa have something in common: They're four-sided. That means that they can go anywhere in the center of a room and you don't have to conceal one side against a wall. Also a desk is a tall, leggy piece of furniture that helps offset the heaviness of the upholstered pieces in a group.

Another major wooden piece that could be used in a conversation group is a worktable. Generally larger than a desk, it's usually thirty-two inches to thirty-six inches wide, seventy-two inches long and normal height, which is twenty-nine to thirty inches. A worktable is not only an interesting piece, it's very versatile. When a room is in a state of repose the worktable serves as a likely spot for an attractive display of accessories, but it can be rearranged for dining. It's also a work area, like a desk, for special projects or study or work brought home from the office. Worktables can be any period from seventeenth century to something made of corrugated cardboard that is right for the Saturday Generation (you'll meet the Saturday Generation after a few pages). Worktables can be of any material, from steel and glass to the most elegant traditional woods. But, be it a desk or a worktable, every room needs one.

Another possible major wooden piece in a room would be a console table. A console table can have many shapes. It might be a half-round table thirty-six inches long; it might be a rectangular table approximately the same size. But by a console table I mean a table some six feet long (some custom-made examples can be even longer). The console table can be used behind a sofa in a length compatible with the length of the sofa, that is, three or four inches shorter on either end.

A console table is a marvelous place to put an important lamp, balanced by perhaps another lamp at one end of the sofa. I dislike, generally, having a pair of lamps, one at either end of the sofa. It's been done too much, and though it's practical in some rooms, it's not a particularly exciting arrangement because it becomes too heavy a balance element *within* a conversation group.

These wooden and upholstered pieces can be combined in all the ways described above to create the conversation group, and all balanced within the group 50/50. Now we have composed one of the major units in a room. Where do we put it? Let's stop and consider the use of the room.

Since the living room is the room with the most traffic and population, let's consider how you use yours. Let's assume that your living room is going to be used mainly by your family and immediate friends and only infrequently for enormous parties, where you must have lots of free space for, say, one hundred guests at a stand-up cocktail party. Inveterate party-givers need to allow for that kind of traffic and space. In the ordinary apartment or house, a living room is used mostly by its inhabitants. If you do occasionally throw a party for a hundred, you'll find—as I do—that the guests may feel a little cramped and eventually end up scattered through every room in the house. That's all right. It's cozy and intimate, and people in small conversation groups all over the house seem to have a good time.

Fundamentally, I think that a room is more attractive when most of the space is filled up—and I don't mean cluttered up. Instead of having a great open space at the center of the room created by having most of the furniture all around the perimeter (dull) I much prefer to put the conversation grouping of major upholstered pieces and their companion wooden pieces in the center of the room—as a seating island bounded by the perimeter.

But *where* in the center of the room? That depends on the second point of balance in your room—either an architectural element or an equally important arrangement of furniture somewhere else in the room.

When your second balance point is architectural, it is, by its very nature, non-upholstered and offsets the visual weight of the upholstered group. So you don't have anything architectural in your room—it's just a modern box. What about that second balance area? Create it.

Usually you will want your second balance point to be at the perimeter of a room. It should start with something fairly large and important and not upholstered. Like a big armoire or a large commode with a beautiful mirror or painting over it.

A personal note: Even though there is more and more a trend away from completely traditional French furniture, and a movement toward the modern and traditional mix, I still believe, mixed or not, there is nothing as beautiful as an authentic Louis XV commode with a smashing ornate mirror over it. For me, this is a very dramatic combination for a room

—even when there *is* an architectural balance point in the room.

In a more contemporary room, the second balance point could be a fabulous console table completely clad in stainless steel or polished chrome. Or a fabulous wall unit—a combination of shelves and storage. Or your second balance point could be a combination of a console table and a big painting.

Art is very focal, and a good piece or a collection of pieces of sculpture on an authoritative pedestal (or group of pedestals) could serve as a splendid balance point in any kind of room, traditional or modern.

The Perimeter of the Room

Once you have arrived at your two major points of balance—an upholstered conversation group and either an architectural or a composed area of grandeur, you come to the pieces of furniture that can be placed on the perimeter of the room. These could be a commode, an armoire, a credenza, a series of étagères, a library cabinet or other storage pieces. Generally, for me, the only pieces of furniture that *must* be against the walls are pieces that do not have a finished back. I tend to place anything that has four finished sides out into the room.

I have said the perimeter of the room and not the *walls* of the room. All furniture needs space around it.

If a console table, for example, is to be on the edge of a room, where space is available, I prefer to set it about nine to ten inches away from the wall so that there is air around it. A painting hanging on the wall above a console table that is placed away from the wall is hanging behind the table, not directly above it. It's a more pleasing arrangement. Even if I place a console table behind a sofa I always leave air around it.

Sometimes, when others are putting furniture in a room for me, I find everything jammed together—the end tables smack up against the sides of the sofa, the console table pushed up against the back. I always move the furniture and separate pieces at least six inches so that each piece floats, has it's own place in space. For me, it's visually right.

So far we have discussed the basic principle of furniture choice and arrangement for living rooms. The same is true for any other room in your house or apartment. The principles are the same:

1. Consider the necessary elements for the room.

2. Figure out the one major element in the room.

3. Balance that major element with another —either architectural or created with another furniture group.

4. Balance the upholstered pieces with equal weight in hard surfaces, be they wood, metal or plastic.

This balance in a room is probably the one thing that has led me to believe that all rooms should have a double purpose. In a dining room I like a seating group somewhere for balance. This way the vast wood of a dining table is offset by a small group of, say, a love seat and two chairs (space permitting).

If I have a forte it is the bed-sitting room. I have done literally hundreds of them. Again, there is that possibility for the two balance areas: The big, upholstered, soft area of the bed, and somewhere else in the room a conversation group of a desk, an open arm chair, and an armoire. Always there are the two

balance points: A group of upholstery (soft) and another group of wooden pieces (hard).

That reduces decoration to a formula, and is perhaps oversimplifying because there are so many decisions to be made within the arrangement of the two major elements in a room, but I think it will be helpful to you in organizing your thinking when it comes to planning your own model room—the one you'll be living in.

Now for the Floor Plan

If you've followed my theory of design so far, you have an idea of what your room is like and have drawn a room plan to scale. You have considered what the two basic points of balance in the room will be. You have ascertained what elements will go into each of these areas. You have thought about what peripheral arrangements you would like. Now it's time to see if you can make them work in your room.

I suggest using tracing paper and furniture templates. "Templates" is nothing but a fancy term for paper cut outs of furniture drawn in the same scale as your room plan.

You make templates of the furniture that you have and are going to keep for your room—after carefully measuring and drawing them to scale before cutting them out. (The cardboard that comes from the laundry with shirts is perfect for this purpose because you're going to be tracing the outlines of the templates.)

In addition to the furniture you already have, make a list of the pieces you must look for and buy to fill out the room. Imagine the approximate size they must be, do scale drawings of them and cut out templates. But don't be too firm about the size. Cut out more things than you need. Cut out a longer sofa and a shorter sofa, two sofas, two love seats, several sizes of chairs.

Now put your room plan on a work surface and place a sheet of tracing paper over it. Place the templates in an arrangement you think might work, and draw their outlines on the tracing paper. Then, another tracing paper and another combination. Keep doing it. Then put your tracings out on a table and compare them all. Soon you'll arrive at the one that pleases you most (or that you would like to show to a professional for possible further refinement).

You now have organized your thinking to the point where you know something about the scale of the furniture, the arrangement and, most important, the balance.

Now all you have to decide is what the furniture will look like: Traditional, modern or mix.

This is a traditional banquette arranged in an L shape for this particular setting—although in other settings it could be a large-scale U. Not only does such a banquette make an architectural statement, it's also extraordinarily comfortable. It's accented by a steel-and-glass table and what I think is the ultimate in modern box furniture—a dark brown laminated commode with a high-gloss finish. There's more gloss in the lacquered walls. This banquette derives its traditional look from the plush velvet upholstery. But if you wanted a banquette to look contemporary it could be covered with any number of other fabrics. I can recommend the use of banquette seating not only for comfort but for great flexibility in design and mood.

This is another version of the banquette that is very simple and quite contemporary. Here, all the seating is armless chair units used in conjunction with architectural elements and matching tables. The bases of these chair units are aluminum, surfaced to look like brushed stainless steel, which contrasts nicely with the texture of the woolen suiting upholstery in a rich nutmeg color.

So, you see, the banquette can look very traditional or very slick, depending on the fabric and the environment of the whole room.

Although the arrangement of furniture here is quite classic, the room setting requires an explanation. This model room was based on a Thai house in Bangkok, which accounts for the window shapes, the use of wood paneling and the absence of panes in the windows. In Thailand the rain always comes from one direction, and that side of a Thai house is protected by a tremendous deck and overhang. The other three sides have windows without panes, which allow for maximum cross ventilation. But even though the setting is exotic, the furniture arrangement is classic: A camelback sofa upholstered in a patterned Siamese silk fabric and the traditional wing chair are grouped with a pair of open-arm bamboo chairs in deep brick red to blend with the brick red, green and lavender of the silk upholstery fabric.

Here the furniture arrangement is focused on a window. The pair of sofas are upholstered in a very neutral color of Siamese silk and placed with a pair of open arm chairs upholstered in a similar color in suede. These face a large square cocktail table to form a grouping for easy conversation. The texture of the suede makes a very attractive foil for the shine of the Siamese silk and the neutral tones of the Indian chain-stitch rug. Note the oversize figure on the cocktail table.

This is a highly sophisticated mix of weights, textures and mass. Achieving a balance is a little tricky. First you need to understand that there is unusual strength in the colors of the room, not evident in this black-and-white photo. The walls are painted intense red. The sofa is upholstered in lilac-colored wool. The colors of the supergraphics on the wall are a deeper shade of red than the walls, the lilac of the upholstery, plus a deeper tone of lilac, and magenta. You might call the combination vibrant. Against this background the lightness of the plexiglass chairs, the massiveness of the Louis XIII armoire, the bulk of the plexi-glass cube used as a cocktail table, the chrome legs on the sofa and the mirrored chrome cube all provide enough variation to make a balance possible. The plexiglass chairs are arranged so that you can see *through* them to the armoire. In order to balance the weight of the sofa I used a larger-than-usual open arm chair. To balance the austerity of the Louis XIII armoire I used an equally austere smoky plexiglass cube. The simple glint of the chrome lamp balances the chrome legs of the sofa and the mirrored chrome cube. Though it's quite a mix, when the balances are carefully thought out it works.

This is a guest bed-sitting room, and so instead of a sofa, the major upholstered piece is a daybed. That's why the lamp table is in front of it instead of at the side—the usual arrangement with a sofa. The ends of the daybed are much too high to give easy access to the table, and if you're stretched out on the daybed the source of light and the table are right at hand. But the furniture is classically arranged: Adjacent to the daybed, a pair of steel-and-brass campaign chairs with natural leather sling backs; and across from that group a trestle-based campaign desk and a Louis XIII open arm chair in leather to take the place of a wing chair. The island is all held together by the Oriental rug. By the way, those beautifull steel-and-brass étagères built into the niches have shelves upholstered in natural leather.

This living room is done in Louis XIII style, and illustrates another classic arrangement. Because of the heaviness and bulk of the furniture, instead of having a pair of chairs at one end of the sofa, I've used a pair of wing chairs opposite one another for balance. Opposite the sofa is a bench upholstered with matching fabric, while on the diagonal are a Louis XIII table desk and open arm chair, with typically heavy, bulbous turned legs. You'll see that the profiles of the lamps in the room are at the same height even though the tables they're standing on are not. Elsewhere we have talked about the use of lambrequins as window treatment, and here is an example.

This is a variation in arrangement. The sofa is set into a niche lit with downlights, balanced with a pair of Empire open arm chairs in matching fabric and a desk out in the center of the room with a chair in the same fabric. The bulk of the entire upholstered grouping is offset by the free-standing étagère. A word about the color in this arrangement. The wall covering is cream patent vinyl printed in three shades of apricot and peach, while the major upholstery is in peach-colored velvet, the smaller chairs in matching linen.

These Louis XV pieces were all meticulously reproduced from pieces in a museum in the south of France and are typical of the area. The buffet, or *bahut*, has a hutch top, or *vais-selier.*The setting is a kitchen-dining room, and the arrangement balances the dining group-ing, the big, plumply cushioned rush-seat chair and the *bahut*.

A worktable can be built in, as you see it here, rather than standing free. In this case, I wanted the worktable to be an organic part of the room, and so it's built to emerge from the wall and underscore the molded shapes of the room.

I have often stressed the importance of desks and worktables in a furniture grouping, and this is a beautiful example: A black lacquer Louis XV desk. It's very formal yet surprisingly simple, even with the ormolu mounts of bronze doré on the corners and the superb banding around the edge. You can find hundreds of tables in this design, mostly with a great deal more ornamentation. I chose this one because it's such a fine example. The same could be said of the Louis XV burl wood commode in the corner. I much prefer these simple classic pieces to the opulent furniture used in court settings. Note the use of many, many boxes as decorative accessories.

I would call this a perfect corner for contemplation and work. In a cave setting this modern version of a sawhorse table in polished chrome with a thick slab of glass for the top is light, airy, and suitable to the mood of the room. This entire work area is a still life arrangement of furniture, sculptural forms and accessories, from the tall plexiglass étagère and the plexiglass column supporting an admirable piece of sculpture right down to the accessories on the worktable. The sleekness of all these is toned down by the Alaskan sheepskin rug and pillows.

This is another splendid example of a metal-and-glass worktable. Here the supports are made of brushed brass. In company with the Louis XIII arm chair, it balances the weight of the armoire.

13/traditional or modern?

There is much to choose from in furniture styles. One of the traditional periods may be for you. For me, the possibilities in seventeenth-century period furniture—either English, French, Italian or Spanish (all with similarities in style)—are enormously appealing. Pieces from this period can be placed in an environment that is strictly seventeenth century or mixed with the most modern designs. The large proportions of furniture from this period makes it a perfect foil in a very, very modern setting.

A more formal look can be found in beautifully and delicately carved Regence French pieces—early eighteenth century. You can use furniture of the Regence period in an all-French environment or mix it with Parsons-type tables that have been lacquered or covered with suitable fabric, or as a contrast with many choice modern pieces. When I say a total French environment, I don't mean a museum re-creation—I mean an up-to-date French look with contemporary accessories, color scheme and placement of furniture.

There Is No Such Thing as French Provincial

The next period you might consider is Louis XV, recognized by curved cabriole legs. I am particularly fond of the Louis XV furniture that was made in the provinces and which is commonly thought of as country French furniture.

Let me clear up a common misconception. There really is no such thing as French Provincial. Every province of France (and areas of other European countries as well) has its own distinctive style, whether it's north, south, east, west or central France. Climatic considerations contribute to give each area its particular look. I know, we think of certain commercial furniture as being typical of "French Provincial," but that is not true at all.

If you go to the north of France, to Brittany, the furniture has very austere, severe lines. This furniture is much closer to the seventeenth century in style. Then, if you move down to Provence, which is the extreme opposite example, you're in a sunny, almost Mediterranean climate. The furniture has very soft, flowing lines with delicate baskets of flowers and little bouquets blooming on the aprons and the drawer fronts.

Each province has a very distinctive furniture style because the pieces made by local craftsmen were usually a more primitive interpretation of what was being used in the grand palaces and villas. However, country French furniture has a distinctly different look from the inlaid precious wood, veneered, bronze ormolu mounted elegant furniture that was used in palaces.

I think there is very little room in today's living for the elegant court styles. The country styles are eminently more adaptable to life in America—either in an authentic (though modernized) setting, or as one element of a mix with more contemporary furniture.

From the seventeenth century on, you can easily identify almost any period by its legs. Louis XV furniture has curved cabriole legs. Here we have the earliest and simplest version —a country table with a Regence leg terminating in a hoof foot. Later in the century many forms of the cabriole leg, with varying degrees of carving, depending on whether they originated in the country or the city, were to be found.

This is an outrageous use of metal. The dining table is a hoof foot Regence and very country. And, mixed with it, Directoire-style polished steel chairs from France (part of a whole collection of garden furniture that, normally, would be lacquered white—I like it in plain metal that has been highly polished). The silvery, lustrous metal is very compatible with the patina of the wood in the table. All the lamps in the room are done in polished steel, too. The accessories are all polished pewter. Outrageous though it may be, metal accents do enhance a traditional room.

Following Louis XV came Louis XVI period characterized by round or square tapered legs with fluting. Slightly later came the Directoire period—a transitional period in which studied simplicity was the order. Legs were stripped of fluting and though they were either round or square, they always had an understated, quiet formality. At the very beginning of the nineteenth century was the Empire period, which in its simpler forms became even more understated. Here we have Louis XVI chairs, library cabinet and commode, a Directoire desk, and Empire pot table and daybed. This is a very harmonious gathering of periods without everything matching.

Chronologically, the next period is Victorian. One of the styles that was transitional during this period and is very much in use today is furniture constructed of turned bamboo. Modern interpretations of this style—late nineteenth century—can be used in many ways. I'm particularly fond of it when it's lacquered in white or bright colors. It's very effective when combined with mirror or metal and glass, or with most solid lacquered furniture—something akin to the Parsons table. Furniture made of real bamboo seems very right for the informality of today's casual style of living.

After the bamboo styling of the last century, the only period is modern—which means as many things as there are modernists to define it.

This chapter is not meant to be a textbook on every kind and period of furniture that exists in the world. It is intended only to suggest some forms and styles of furniture that I have used through the years and have found very livable—particularly when they're arranged in a timely style. Period isn't all. It's how it's used.

You may have noticed that when I speak of mixing periods, I usually refer to *two* types only. For example, I'll say seventeenth century and modern, but not seventeenth century, Louis XV and modern. In my own home, I have mixed many things together, but I've had a lot of experience. Although there are many exponents of mixing all the styles you can as long as they pass the test of being basically well designed, I think this can be hazardous. The amateur can't balance all the pros and cons of a varied mix. It's extremely difficult to make it come off. What usually results is a hodgepodge. If you feel that you truly want a mixed bag in decoration, leave the doing to a professional.

Pulling It All Together

So far, we've suggested the kinds of furniture you might consider. We've also (hopefully) started you thinking about the kinds of pieces you will need for your room. Here's a footnote: Scale is very important in a room. Elsewhere I have discussed the two balance points, the two big groups of furniture you need in a room arrangement. Scale is another form of room balance and it relates to the *height* and bulk of architecture and furniture in a room.

I usually like one tall piece of furniture. It serves as a balance for high features in a room, like tall windows, and especially doors. Every room has at least one door. It's just a big aperture that leads to another room. To balance a door opening you can use draperies at a window, or some contemporary arrangement with blinds.

I feel that you need further emphasis on height in a room. I like a credenza with a very impressive mirror over it. Or a table with a big painting. Or a line-up of storage pieces. Or you can cover most of a wall with a grouping of paintings. Or one big piece of supergraphics.

14/accents in metal furniture

Anyone who wants to brighten up a room that is predominantly traditional can do it easily, quickly and relatively inexpensively and give a whole new lift to a room. Metal furniture.

Into a traditional room introduce a brass-and-smoky-glass cocktail table, for instance. Or brass étagères. Brass, polished chrome or brushed chrome can be added to almost any room. The guide to the selection of the color of the metal you use is in the accessories you have in the room. If you have a lot of polished brass accessories, then use polished brass in furniture. Take a brass étagère with glass shelves. The glitter of the glass and the glow of the brass give a real lift to any room.

By the way: You can enhance such an étagère by putting one of the new can spot-lights on the floor below the glass shelves. The light that shines up through them will cast graceful shadows on the ceiling and at the same time light up everything on the shelves.

In a very contemporary design use glass-and-metal pieces mixed with traditional. If you prefer the pure traditional, here is a look you will like. This room is in shades of black, gray and tobacco. The étagère, with its smoky glass shelves and brass frame, is very effective against the deep-toned wall.

124

Go all the way to total metal. This is a very advanced look in modern architecture. I like the glaze of the walls and ceiling that have been lacquered to a shine as dazzling as the finish on a new car. Further shine comes from the lighted plexiglass windows. Then there's the metallic glimmer of metal furniture, metal trim around the windows, metal lamp, metal frame on the chair, metal fan-shaped storage unit and container for the softness of a plant.

I think this room shows quite graphically that there is a place for everything in decoration. There's a place for traditional and there's a place for the super-new. This is not a room for everyone, but it's an exciting interpretation of a very modern look.

This room combines everything. It's got traditional tuxedo-style upholstered furniture, a pair of black chinoiserie side chairs and an overall feeling of traditional charm. And yet, we have used a pair of small cocktail tables in brushed nickel with mirror tops. And, in addition, there are pedestals in mirror chrome. They have doors that close for concealed storage, but their most important function is to support those great urns with flower arrangements. The pedestals could also be used as bases for sculpture. By the way, the walls in this room are of shiny, gun-metal patent vinyl applied like thick, fat upholstery.

Steel, steel, and more steel: Here a pierced metal-top table and armchair in traditional French garden furniture—but untraditional in its lack of paint, and highly polished instead. The use of metal is further compounded by a Gothic turned metal candlestick with a metal bouillotte shade.

15/the saturday generation

That's what we call them at Bloomingdale's, but they're everywhere—all over the country, all over the world. We call them the Saturday Generation because they fill our stores on Saturdays. They're young, they're vital, they're hardworking. And Saturday is about the only day they have to shop.

Maybe you're a member of the Saturday Generation. If so, we know you. Some of you have gone to work right from high school or trade school. Some of you are just starting out in your profession. You may have a roommate, you may be newly married, you may live in a bachelor pad. You're informed, you've got taste (usually more taste than money, right?) and as far as today is concerned, you're with it.

And because your means are limited, you have to find ways to decorate your apartment without professional help and still have snappy, happy surroundings. Time was when the bachelor pad was nothing more than a dingy studio couch that served for sitting as well as sleeping, a "something" to store things in and a few travel posters tacked on the wall. No more.

There are foam rubber modular seating units in unusual shapes covered with serviceable cotton fabrics. (Who's got the time for constant maintenance or the money for domestic help?)

There are molded plastic tables, chairs and étagères that come in all colors—from black to white to the brilliant hues of orange, yellow, blue and green in between. The colors can be used together or you can go subtle in all-white.

There are molded plastic desks that take up no more room than a small table, and yet hold everything a young student or beginning professional needs.

Unpainted furniture comes in a great variety of styles, from modern to country French. There are furniture pieces that are turned to look like bamboo. These natural wood pieces can be finished any way, from a high-shine lacquer to a warm satiny finish. Too, they can be mixed with sleek plastic pieces. One of my favorite wooden pieces is a contemporary copy of a French farmhouse table that looks as good in its natural state as it does painted or lacquered.

Just because the space you live in is limited doesn't mean you have to put up with sparse furnishings. Do you entertain a lot? You need chairs. I love the new stacking chairs. They're beautifully designed as individual chairs, but they look like a piece of sculpture when stacked in a corner, where they become a splendidly designed architectural column.

Since many apartments are one-room arrangements, bedroom furniture just doesn't work. The bed that's slept on at night must serve for seating during the day. Today you can find wonderful platform beds that are island couches in the daytime and great beds at night. There are tremendous varieties of designs for couches that convert to beds.

Certainly, in one room you need storage space for items that would normally be in a bedroom. In today's stores there are plenty of chests, trunk baskets and multiple-drawer furniture for storage.

Fortunately, some of today's best designers are devoting their talents to furniture that is contemporary looking, can be mass produced and consequently is in the right price range for the new homemaker with a slim budget.

A bit of advice, however. Furniture for you of the Saturday Generation is not dime-store cheap. But neither is it anywhere as expensive as conventionally constructed furniture. Generally, it is well made and durable enough to last until a young couple is making a little more money. The trick to finding the best of this furniture is to look for clean lines. The better manufacturers keep their products uncluttered. Others might mask inferior furniture with fancy trim that could obscure shoddy workmanship and material. One good rule of thumb is to buy furniture from a reliable store that assures you of good quality in the first place, and backs it with their reputation.

So, if you belong to the Saturday Generation, that doesn't mean you have to be Saturday's child. Quality and taste abound in furniture with zip and personality.

All towers and all smashing. Red, red, red. All these towers are made of two component parts. They are combo units, meant for storage. On the left you see two of the units, consisting of a smaller cylinder that sits on a larger drum. The two are sold as a set, but you can buy set after set after set and do a whole room in them, as here. That means that the whole room becomes storage space. The units can also be used as little rolling bars because they do have hidden casters. Or they can be grouped as cocktail tables, or as architectural support for a desk top. Here, I just combined the units in their many ways and arranged them on a matching red plexiglass floor.

Dark brown plastic in a series of modular units that can be snapped together to form walls, ledges, shelves, tables, consoles, coffee tables—almost anything your imagination permits. Here the units are used to form a very special environment. This is an all-purpose room. The walls are metal mesh, which contrasts in texture with the slickness of the dark brown plastic. The accessories in the room are mainly chrome. The total room is one of textures and different kinds of shine—with a touch of African art for accent.

All white plastic and naturals. These are the same modular units used in the brown plastic room. They snap together—you can see the crack lines that identify the shape of the units. They're mixed with natural woods—the Finnish table has a butcherblock top; the natural wood chairs have rush seats. The only other element in the room is straw—straw rug and straw accessories. If you decide that you're bored with the arrangement, you can take apart all the components and snap them together into something totally different. And that's the fun of it.

Would you believe cardboard! To me, this is the most fantastic development in furniture today. It's beautifully constructed, beautifully designed and sculpted. It's all made of corrugated cardboard. Everything: Walls, floor, beds, table, chairs. It's very warm and very beautiful, and still has a very monastic feeling. This furniture is Saturday Generation. It's a new understated and stylish use for an old material.

Nothing could be simpler than this furniture. But the setting, the arrangement and the use of a multi-level platform give it a feeling of distinction. This furniture would do just as well in the room of a young person still living at home or in a bachelor pad. But the same furniture could easily be used in a far more sophisticated environment, and it would still be admirable because of its cleanness of line and elegance of design.

The Saturday Generation abroad. Talking about painted furniture, here it is. This is a collection of very provincial French furniture. It's heavy and rustic and comes ready to be painted in any color you want and can think of. It can fit into a contemporary or a severe setting. This room could be a garret or a beach house in the south of France. This is a very good example of stylish unpainted furniture.

Frill-less furniture. This is a fine example of furniture that is well designed and totally without frills. What's more, it is well priced. It can be used in a variety of ways for a variety of purposes. Here you see it arranged in a student's room. The window treatment is a device to disguise a bad window, or create the appearance of a window in a wall that doesn't have one.

A mirror room. Done entirely in mirror and white. The only color is in the double-decker bed, which is brilliant orange. The furniture is beautifully designed. The chair in the center is the now famous bean-bag chair. The furniture to the left is a pair of chests that look as though they were a dresser but are individual units that could fill a whole wall. The lines are clean, the look totally uncluttered.

16/beds

The Glorious Four-Poster

I love a four-poster bed because of the way it dominates a room and fills in the air space over the bed. A plain bed just plopped in a room becomes a great mass of upholstery. So much blank space above a bed always bothers me. Too, I tend to like things that have a built-in look and a sense of architecture to them—a coziness, a feeling of containment.

Here is an example of a very heavily turned post on a bed in a room setting that is very seventeenth century. Because of the massiveness of the bed, I chose to treat it in a relatively simple way with very heavy, strongly patterned fabric. The room is weighty architecturally, and, in my mind, it just didn't call for a lot of drapery.

Here is a totally different example. This is a daybed which is actually a convertible sofa that opens into a queen-size bed. I hung a canopy of Siamese silk from the ceiling on chains, and from the inside of the canopy hung draperies to enclose the bed. The result is a French country sitting room which can easily convert into a guest room.

This is a great Spanish spindle bed—queen size, which is five feet—with traditional Spanish manta bedspreads, just as they are woven, used both on the bed and as a canopy. For the canopy, all I did was cut holes in the corners, drape it over the top of the bed, put the finials back on, and—voilà!—a primitive treatment for the four-poster. The bed is heavy enough so that it didn't need corner draperies.

Another country French bedroom with walls completely covered in shirred, pongee-colored, lightweight linen. The walls, the slanted and flat parts of the ceiling and in between the beams are covered with fabric. The only apparent woodwork is the beams that give space separation to the room. The fabric is shirred on all the wall space between these beams. The bed treatment is rather elaborate. The bed has only a painted wooden headboard in an antique pongee color. The bed canopy is cantilevered off the back wall and attached to the beam. The shirred valance fits in with the whole shirred decor of the room. It's a canopy bed effect without a canopy bed.

You can either have a four-poster bed and drape it—simply or elaborately—or you can pretend that you have a four-poster by hanging a valance from the ceiling or cantilevering it off the wall and using one of the vast array of drapery treatments.

I have included this photo here because although not strictly traditional, it is not starkly modern either. The simple raw wood posts of the bed, the raw wood dowel sticks on the wall, and the natural color of the bedspread lends a warmth that makes the room "transitional" for those who like a middle line between traditional and modern.

This is a beautiful brass four-poster bed from England. I have used this bed in larger-sized rooms and have draped it with voluptuous folds of fabric. But I feel that occasionally beds are beautiful enough to stand alone in a room—particularly in this room where the architecture is so strong that a heavily draped bed would be out of place. Here, instead of a bedspread, I have used an antique Oriental rug as a bed cover—with stacks of all kinds of pillows in velvets, silks and embroidery that blend with the colors of the rug.

A simpler treatment: A twisted-post bed with an elaborate back panel and a straight valance. You can use shaped or plain valances. It depends on the style. I feel that on a Louis XV bed it's possible to follow the curves that are part of the bed design and shaped valances are suitable. But for the seventeenth century which is more apt to have straight, angled paneling, it makes more sense to have a straight, severely tailored valance. The quilted bedspread, again with quilting done in long channels stuffed with Dacron padding to give a softer feeling.

This is a child's room. Here I built an architectural detail into the room. I made the bed look built-in by dropping the ceiling over it and running crown molding around the dropped portion as if it were a part of the room construction. The ceiling drop is three inches wider and longer than the measurements of the bed. The valance is attached to the underside of this overhead soffit, and tie-back draperies form an enclosure for the bed. If the bed and draperies were taken away, all you'd have is a big niche in the corner. But this way, a bed niche has been created and makes a much more exciting room for a little girl. The bed itself is nothing more than a mattress and springs with a little painted headboard.

Billowing white batiste—yards and yards and yards of it, surrounding a four-poster brass bed.

Cupboard beds are traditionally French, generally found in great farmhouse kitchens where the farm laborers slept—or in some cases, a member of the household. This is a contemporary rendition of a cupboard bed built into a corner of a room and placed on a platform to give it a slight feeling of seclusion. The contour of the built-in part of the bed is repeated in the very simple treatment of the flat valance. The narrow tieback draperies are quite full. I think cupboard beds are great things for a country house, and I hope the idea never gets lost.

A Word About Bedspreads

For very practical as well as esthetic reasons, bedspreads should always be quilted. Whether they're done in the most beautiful, fragile Siamese silks or in heavy woolens.

If it's a bedspread that comes on and off the bed every day, quilting is a foolproof way to avoid wrinkles. A quilted bedspread can be folded very easily. The next day it's as smooth as when you took it off. Quilting helps bedmaking, too. A quilted spread just sort of plops into place with a minimum of effort because it's firm. And you don't have to fuss to make it smooth. Plus: A quilted spread helps to smooth over and fill out the irregularities of blankets and sheets and gives the bed a softer look.

I prefer big, puffy quilting as plump as a comforter. After all, a bed displays a large expanse of fabric, and quilting helps to break it up. So not only is quilting practical, but it's a very pretty way to decorate a bed.

The Spatial Contemporary Bed

When it comes to contemporary settings, I completely contradict my remarks on the four-poster. Instead of beds in enclosures, I like the complete openness, the sparse look of a platform bed. A modern bedroom does not call for a heavily filled-in space. I like the great open spaces and large expanses of air.

This bed is made all of corrugated cardboard. As contemporary as it is, in a sense it harks back to the Gothic period—a bed built-up on a platform and headed by a baldachino—a canopy over altars and thrones in many churches. If you look closely, you'll see that the headboard cantilevers slightly outward from the wall creating a demi-canopy. There was no intent to create a Gothic architectural design in this room—it was meant to be freshly contemporary. And yet it echoes the past. The effect is, quite simply, smashing.

The platform for this island bed is made of translucent plexiglass and lit from the inside with fluorescent bulbs. The mattress nestles into the platform. And in contrast to the slickness and brightness of the plexiglass . . . a fur bedspread. Worth noting: The walls. They're hung, wall-to-wall, with nothing but white plastic beads that cover even the window opening, which you can just barely see on the left-hand side of the photo. The shine of the beads combined with the white vinyl floor and the plexiglass is enormously effective. The beads are hung in strings from behind a soffit all around the ceiling. When there are air currents in the room, there is just the slightest shimmer of movement on the walls. Very pretty.

Here is the simplest of platform beds—a riser inside of which is a plain metal spring which supports a mattress. Here, it is used as an island bed in the center of a room. The lighting is brought to the bed instead of being placed against the wall.

Transitional approach to a bedroom. The wallpaper is a contemporary adaptation of the flame stitch, which is a seventeenth-century design, here worked out in contemporary colors. The bed is a combination of steel and wood—a modern interpretation of the four-poster. Although the furniture is straight-line modern, the look is far from clinical. Much of the warmth and feeling of shelter comes from the canopy that fills the air space above the bed.

The simplest possible four-poster, here interpreted in sleek stainless steel—very simple, very straightforward. With it, a mixture of wooden and stainless steel furniture. The trampoline canopy intensifies the spareness. The walls are completely covered with white, shiny beads.

A final word: In a bedroom the bed should be important. In traditional rooms I like beds that are either four-poster or made to look that way. In contemporary rooms the beds should have importance because of the space they occupy. Just to stick a bed into a room has no effect whatsoever. If style is the name of the game (and it is!) the bed must be the core from which the excitement of style emanates.

17/dining

Dinner Is Served

Dining is one of my favorite activities. And, as a designer, I am very much interested in the subject of dining *rooms*. Let's consider a few that I have done in the model rooms. There should certainly be something here that will serve as inspiration for you when it comes time to plan your dining area—for these rooms illustrate all the changes from ultra-primitive to super-contemporary.

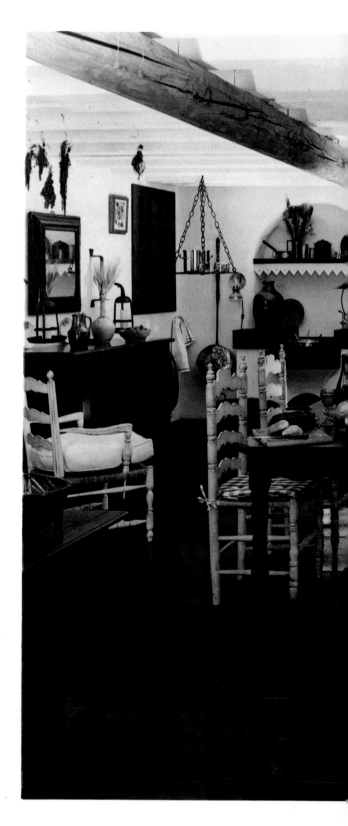

This very rustic kitchen was influenced by a typical room in a provincial museum in Bayonne in the southern part of France. We chose particular pieces and had them reproduced, line for line. Granted, not everyone would want to be this authentic, and there is certainly a lot going on in it—it's like an Early American keeping room. But it's a fun way to dine.

An Early American trestle table dominates this room. It's eight feet long and the top is all one piece. It can be used for dining, as a worktable, or as a console table, and wouldn't necessarily have to go in a dining area. The strength of the design makes it able to stand alone. You don't look at it and say, "It's a dining table." In a room as multi-purpose as this one, the dominant table should be versatile.

A more sophisticated version of country dining: The French dough-box table was originally used for baking. The top would lift up, allowing the housewife to knead and store her bread dough. This is a reproduction of an authentic piece, supplied with a larger top to give knee space. With it are claw-and-ball-foot Spanish chairs.

A touch of England—all the furniture being typical of what you would find in an English country cottage, re-created here with beam-and-straw ceiling and timbered walls. The Windsor chairs are typical of those used in homes, taverns and pubs in England, as is the large seventeenth-century oval table with round, turned legs. I love the open Welsh dresser that can be used for serving and for the storage of pewter tankards and old English Staffordshire pottery.

This shows one end of a very early, very primitive American keeping room—an all-purpose room that even has a bed in it. I am very fond of this rustic provincial look—as the photos in this book amply show—from American to Spanish to English to French. The very word "dining" seems to imply a certain formality, but dining need not be stiff, as rooms like this indicate.

The atmosphere here is country, but less primitive. The table is country French, but the chairs are polished steel—also from France. They're actually adaptations of garden furniture that probably would have been lacquered white. But for this effect, we asked the manufacturer to polish the steel. The glitter of the chairs is a lovely complement to the fruitwood of the table. The approach to country dining here is much more sophisticated than the more authentic provincial look.

In this cave atmosphere the dining table is built-in and the chairs around it are contemporary versions of country ladderback chairs: Just a simple ladder and a rush seat. The background is very austere, and, because of that, very fresh.

Here is a category of furniture that bridges the gap between traditional and modern. The table is an elaborate version of the Parsons type with reeded legs done in bright, shiny yellow lacquer. It's large enough to seat six people comfortably and eight cozily. This is a very clean, today approach to decorating not only a dining room but any room in your house—clear, bright colors and furniture that is simple in line. Even the chairs—although they have crisscross latticework set into them—are fairly straightforward.

The simplest possible table sets a supermodern mood for dining. It has a white plexiglass cylinder base and a top of white marble streaked with gray. The understated chairs look almost like tractor seats. They're made of white lacquered tubular metal with a small upholstered seat and back. The look is very sleek, very slick.

This is the ultimate in contemporary dining. The table is totally metal-clad with a brushed aluminum finish. The metal is veneered just like wood. The chairs are upholstered in very pale natural leather. The room is gray, and the sheen of the metal furniture blends in harmoniously.

In a beamed room a dining table that can seat eight is centered before a great white plaster fireplace. This version of a Parsons table has a heavily grained parquet top. You might expect a country style table in this kind of setting, but I love the scale and mood of this up-to-date, beautifully constructed table, and the comfortable upholstered chairs.

Here is dining in a countrified but elegant manner. The typical farm table with ladder-back chairs and benches is placed against a traditional French country background. The paisley print fabric on the walls is taken from old French woodblock patterns.

Best-Dressed Tables

Too often when people set out to decorate a room they think of it in its static state—the way it will look at that instant in time when the last accessory is put in place. They forget about the room as a setting for living; that a room changes mood and appearance as the activity in it changes. No room in a home is more "flowing" than the dining room.

It's used as many as three times a day, and each use is a different kind of event. I'm not talking about the dining *room* as such, I mean the activity that goes on at a dining table wherever it is—indoors or out, whether it's in a New England keeping room that's a combination of living-dining-cooking, or in an area of the living room where you have a dining table. Even if your dining table is used only for dinner and an occasional brunch or luncheon, each meal is different, with different kinds of people, different kinds of food, different times of day, month or year.

And what could be more monotonous than sitting down to the same table with the same china, glassware and silver, meal after meal after meal—family or company.

I believe that eating should be fun. Each meal should be charming and interesting. And it doesn't have to be a big production.

Everyone has a collection of things they love. We all have things like a pair of brass candlesticks picked up at a flea market, a box of shells picked up on a tropical beach, the beginnings of a collection of pre-Columbian art. Use them in table settings. Instead of a conventional centerpiece.

About china and glassware. This is a very subjective thing, but I don't own a complete set of *anything*. I don't have one china service for everything from soup to nuts. I don't have

one set of glassware that will go from cocktails through cordials. I don't use the same flatware for any and every type of food. And I don't have a gravy boat.

Mind you, I love going to friends' homes and sitting down to a beautiful formal dinner with everything matching, and everything thought-out, from the place-card holders to the finger bowls. But I wouldn't like the same theme day after day. And I'm sure my friends don't eat that way every meal, anyway.

My point is: The best-dressed tables are those that have a "wardrobe" of things to go on them. Today's trend is to less formal dining, more casual gatherings for food, more of "drop by" and less of "the pleasure of your company." And because the occasions for dining are different and changing, the way your table looks should be just as versatile. Even in fine department stores, where table settings are on display you will see less and less use of complete sets of china, glassware and silver.

Now, many people already have a complete set of tableware—either they bought it themselves or it was presented to them as a wedding gift. But there is no law that says your present china, serving pieces and glassware can't be combined with other things to give your table variety.

When I say, "I have no sets of anything," I don't mean that my table is hodgepodge. I have an adequate number of dinner plates alike. But the salad plates are different, as are the soup bowls. For example, I have a set of Japanese Imari plates in blue and white. But with them I might use a set of salad plates in rich, orangey red pottery from the south of France.

Tonight I might serve on pottery plates with antique pewter salad plates. Tomorrow night, white plates with an orange and metallic gold border, but the soup bowls might be primitive blue-and-white pottery from Portugal. And the napkins might be a contemporary print on cotton.

The same is true of glass and crystal. The water goblets should be alike. So should the wine glasses—but they should be different from the water goblets. Ditto serving pieces.

Granted, these are very personal tastes, but they may serve to guide you as you accumulate your own table wardrobe.

Like any room in your home, the dining room may have to be a combination of things you already have and new things you'll be buying along the way. Let me tell you about my dining and entertaining to illustrate what I mean by the mix of old and new.

I have a very long, narrow, wooden antique table with beautiful rich graining. Its size makes using a conventional tablecloth out of the question. I love the look of the wood, anyway, and I don't want to hide it with place mats. On special occasions I may decorate it with long runners of antique ribbon or a paisley shawl placed at a rakish angle. But mostly the table is left to look its wooden best without adornment. Many times plates are served in flat baskets to protect the tabletop from heat.

I say that I do not have complete sets of anything, but over the course of the years I have bought things for dining that particularly suit my dining table and the kind of eating and entertaining we do. Not long ago, I found a set of antique green Wedgwood plates that look particularly fine on my wood table. They also go with other things I've had for a long time. What I am doing is buying carefully those things that will go with what I already own and that suit my dining style and that of my guests.

I am fond of baskets. I have baskets and baskets and baskets. I use them as serving units, I use them to hold hot things, I use them for decoration. Some are from Japan, some from Italy, some are American Indian. And I use them as centerpieces, sometimes filled with a loose arrangement of colorful flowers, other times combined with a piece of sculpture I have taken from the armoire, or with a small painting on an easel. I also have a collection of French blue opaline, so a few pieces of that may be used as part of a centerpiece arrangement or, possibly, at one end of the table while four diners are grouped at the other end. My decorations are as unorthodox as my table settings, but they're fun, they make each meal a little unusual.

Even if you tend to be more conventional in your table settings, try to avoid repeating yourself. Make your dining room as changeable as any other room in the house. That way you can run the gamut of moods from gala and festive to warmly informal. You don't have to go to a lot of trouble. Few of us have the time to plan long in advance what our table setting is going to be like, but if you use the things that you have and love in a slightly (or very) unconventional way, you can achieve variety and interest in dining.

The matter of lighting: I happen to believe that nighttime dining should be by candlelight. Lots and lots and lots of candles. Sometimes one large candelabra will be suitable. Other times a cluster of candlesticks of varying heights and sizes will give plenty of light to dine by. Here again, mix as well as match. Gather together candlesticks of various metals —brass, copper, silver, pewter. And mix them on the table. Or mix them with pottery or ceramic holders.

One of the things I like about dining by

candlelight (though I occasionally use antique kerosene lanterns) is that it is not only flattering but it creates a completely different mood from electric light. Because we have no dining room, dinner is served in an area of the living room. During the earlier part of the evening the room is lit by indirect lighting behind statuary and plants and by lamps. Comes time to serve, I light the candles and turn off the lamps, leaving on only the soft indirect lighting. The change of lighting is like going into another room.

All in all, the dining room is the only room in your home that you will be decorating and redecorating every time you sit down to eat, so to help you have a best-dressed table:

Use what you have and want to keep (or must keep for any number of reasons). Then make new purchases that will mix attractively with what you have.

Have enough different types of china, glassware and serving pieces so you can create a different mix as often as you like.

Use the collection of things you have and love—for serving as well as decorating. I have a metal Moroccan pot, originally intended for brewing mint tea. It makes a perfect pitcher for hot syrup for my Sunday morning buttermilk pancakes.

If you like to use tablecloths and place mats, do so. But have a variety and mix them up. Same would be true for napkins. Occasionally, don't put anything on the table, let its natural beauty serve as a background.

Above all, remember that not only must food be delicious to eat and attractive to the eye, it must also be served in an interesting way. Try to achieve as much variety in your table setting as you do in the food you serve. It's not hard once you get away from the conventional ways. And it's fun.

part v/living color

A color scheme will do more than anything else to hold together a miscellaneous assortment of furniture. If you're not able to spend as much as you'd like on new things, your most effective helper in dramatic decorating is *color*. But the right color. Color with impact.

A rich, full-bodied camel-colored paint costs no more than drab buff and might even be available on the same color chart. Vibrant orange-and-white wallpaper costs no more than characterless celadon-and-cream paper. Brightly colored, colorfast cottons are available for slipcovers and draperies at modest prices. So remember—color has no price tag. An inexpensive fabric, dramatic in color *and used lavishly* will do more for a room than a skimpily used expensive fabric—whether the color is right or wrong.

18/how to develop a color sense

What is "right" or "wrong" color? Is it possible for one shade of a color to be beautiful while another tonal value of the same color is, frankly, ugly? There are subtleties in the refinement of colors that require a sophistication of color sense, but you can develop your sense of color and your emotional response to it—and that response is important.

Take orange, for example—orange being one of my favorites. Orange isn't just orange. It can be a thousand colors ranging from yellows just tinged with orange, through pure middle-value orange, to orange with varied amounts of red in it, on to orange that ranges from the palest tint to almost brown.

Now close your eyes and visualize orange in nature: Autumn leaves, California poppies, tulips, zinnias, marigolds, roses, ranunculus, calendula, nasturtiums, cayenne pepper, paprika, carrots, squash, melons, pumpkins, gourds, the color of orange in sunsets, the clay of the Grand Canyon, shells, goldfish, orioles, coral, apricots, peaches, and finally oranges. All of these are orange. To think of them will help to make you relate to orange in a way you would never have thought of before. Study all the other colors in turn until they bring similar pictures to mind. This will force you to think about the infinite variety of each color. You will see and appreciate color harmonies that formerly escaped you. As you become more familiar with color and the dynamics of color combinations you'll find yourself feeling more daring and less intimidated by color. It's daring and excitement in the use of color that can shape the atmosphere that shapes your everyday life.

Another way to learn about color is to visit museums or thumb through art books and see how the great masters used color. I think of the subtlety of colors in paintings by Fra Angelico or Giotto, the softness of a Bonnard, the vibrance of a Matisse. If you look closely at great paintings you'll discover some really surprising uses of color—both as background and as accent.

If the study of paintings seems academic to you, then start a collection of color pictures clipped from good European and American magazines—magazines that have fine color reproduction. Every time you see a picture of a room that has some element you like (colors, architecture, arrangement) clip and save it. Then on some leisurely day, spread all your clippings out on the floor.

You'll be surprised to discover that you're repeating yourself. Many pictures will have the same colors or combinations of colors. You're now beginning to zero in on the colors you like, the colors you'd like to live with. Then start winnowing your collection of clippings. Discard all but the ones that you are really excited about.

There are other sources of inspiration, too. Look at displays in department stores. Certainly not all rooms will be your style, but try to find some use of color that appeals to you. Perhaps you don't like starkly contemporary design, but over there in one corner of a modern room is an interesting use of warm brown combined with rich red-orange. Remember it.

Finally, when it comes time to choose the colors for your room you will have built up a mental reference library from your study of the masters, from looking at all kinds of rooms, and from your clipping file. Then color choices will be amazingly easy for you.

Background Colors: Neutral Does Not Mean Beige

To my mind a neutral is a basic that any accent color will go with. Although people comment on my daring use of color, actually in *most* of the model rooms that I have designed there are no more than three colors used in various textures to lend variety. There are generally two accent colors employed against a neutral background.

If neutral does not mean beige, what does it mean? Several background colors come to mind. Certainly white and off-white. But then there are warm, dark browns, and a color you could call gingersnap (one of my new favorites), or camel, or cinnamon or gray—never a blue-gray, but the deeper tones, from medium gray to charcoal.

Once you have made your choice of background color and the one or two accent colors that will go with it, you are ready to start planning where your colors will go and where to use texture and pattern.

Bear in mind that the style of a room has nothing to do with color. There is no such thing as a "traditional color" or a "modern color." You can see from the color plates in this book that I have used all manner of colors in all manner of rooms. A period room can be done in bright, airy colors, just as a contemporary room can be done in deep, understated tones.

What accent colors can you put against the neutrals? It's a very personal matter. Here are some of my choices. I particularly like the oranges (and keep stating it)—from red-orange to a shade the color of orange sherbet; the yellows, from marigold to chrome yellow; the bright ranges of the greens, from parrot green to poison green; the purples, from lavender to magenta; even blue can be used as an accent color when it's the color of French blue opaline.

Combining Background and Accent Colors

In analyzing the many model rooms that I have done, I can see that my choice and use of colors come down to two basic schemes.

1. Most of the room in one color.

That is, the walls, draperies, curtains, floor covering, and major upholstered pieces (by that I mean a sofa or a banquette and at least one or two additional chairs, depending on the size of the room) all in the same color. Then, for accent, a pair of chairs or other minor upholstery in a secondary color. To this basic scheme you could add third-color accents in such accessories as decorative pillows—certainly the simplest way to introduce accent colors into a room.

A variation on this method might be: Walls, major upholstery, draperies and curtains in one background color, and the secondary color in an area rug. This could be either patterned or solid. Introduce a third color in minor upholstered pieces, and you'll still be able to use additional accent colors in accessories.

2. Monochromatic with a slightly more daring distribution of color.

Use your chosen background color for walls, *minor* upholstered furniture and even the carpeting. Then introduce your secondary color in the *major* pieces of upholstered furniture. When I use the same color on several upholstered pieces I like to have two or three different textures of fabric, including even a subtle pattern. Against these two basic colors you can use an accent color in decorative pillows, art, accessories, flowers.

Balance of color is important, as you can see here, with the majority of the room in soft lemon yellow. A bibliothèque opposite the bed is finished in a dry, antique paint. Adjacent to it a tufted chair in lustrous orange Siamese silk, balanced across the room by a large, draped tablecloth in the same Siamese silk. There are three balance points: The grouping of the chair and bibliothèque; the table; and the additional touch of orange on the bed. The rug combines the orange and yellow with a soft olive green, unifying the whole room.

And yes, you can do an entire room in the same color employing many textures.

The Mary Wells Lawrence Room. Here the highly lacquered walls, the dull-satin upholstery, marble—both real and painted—and the furniture are all in the same tone of color. Variety in texture gives the color strong impact and yet the room is ultra-feminine.

The Truman Capote Room. This is an excellent example of color and pattern balance, using a background color and only two accent colors.

The walls are a cinnamon woolen fabric. (They could well be painted this color or lacquered. You can achieve a very fresh look by using lacquer instead of a flat paint. When the paint is lacquer, the impact of the color doubles in its gloss, its richness, its depth of brilliance.)

The same woolen fabric is used to upholster one important wing chair. The spread on the bed is of red fox fur which repeats the cinnamon tone. Accent color and pattern are introduced in the large-scale paisley of the draperies in cinnamon, deep charcoal, off-white and a rich, orangy red. The charcoal gray is used again in the carpet—in this case broken up with polished chrome strips to keep the expanse of floor from looking too vast in an otherwise intimate room.

Plain or Pattern

Generally speaking, the main living room in a house should have solid color walls in one of the new neutrals listed earlier. Particularly a room that is usually well populated, because people tend to group and form patterns.

In a bedroom or study, where you are apt to spend less time (and more time alone), it's interesting to introduce pattern on the walls. Here are two examples.

Louis XV Bed-sitting Room. Cotton toile of teal blue and cream typical of the eighteenth century cover these walls. Fabric-covered walls were employed then not for their decorative effect alone but to help keep out cold. The bedspread and bed hangings are in natural raw silk, which blends with the wall covering, as does the heavy ribbed faille used to upholster the love seat. A Japanese Tansu chest and the gown in the portrait over the mantel, along with the two velvet pillows, offer the third color accent in the room. The spotted-calf rug is cream and brown to reflect the deep-brown wood tones of the beams and dark wood finish of the bedroom furniture.

The Bill Blass Room. Because this is a bed-sitting room, I liked the idea of bold paisley wallpaper in two shades of orange and a deep apricot against an indigo background. The oranges in the wallpaper are repeated in the bedspread of plaid woolen coating fabric, the apricot tone in the wallpaper is mirrored in the woolen bed hangings. Even though this room is colorful and bold, basically, it is done in only three colors.

The Natural Neutrals

Wood, when used extensively in a room, becomes one of the new neutrals. Here are four examples that show how the natural color of wood can go everywhere.

A country bed-sitting room furnished with imported Italian furniture painted *faux bois*—that is, painted in the traditional way to simulate a new wood finish.

A somewhat grander desert living room with a multiplicity of natural tones: Bleached ash-wood ceiling and ledges, cocoa matting on the floor and traditional rattan in new designs and shapes—all very natural, light and crisp.

In this beach house bleached oakwood is used in a setting composed entirely in the colors of eastern seaboard sand.

All naturals and all whimsical, this room relies on many natural textures, from paper to cocoa matting. Although it doesn't show in this photograph, the wall facing you is lacquered Chinese red in blazing contrast with the many neutrals in the room.

Color that zings. It took its inspiration from a wallpaper that most resembles an Oriental rug, but is definitely updated in colors of cobalt blue, brilliant orange and emerald green—an unexpected combination. In the foreground, a Louis XV bergère in green to balance the matching green on the daybed and in the wall paper. The colors are a gracious welcome to a guest, for this is, in fact, a guest bed-sitting room. The daybed in the center of the room is a surprise. It opens into a queen-size bed and is enclosed by a canopy suspended from the ceiling. An added color touch: The painted floor in orange.

An eighteenth-century room. In this room the black lacquer of the furniture produces the secondary color, with accents of deep apricot repeated in the Louis XV chair, the golden Afghan rug and accessories.

174

An island of rich color. An illustration of the recommended scheme: All of the room is monochromatic except for the major upholstered pieces. Here walls and floor are in a sense the same, but in varying scale, while the upholstered pieces blaze with color.

Sheer drama in the use of color. Terra cotta suede tufted sofa surrounded by large and small accents of Japanese lacquer red combat the strength of the heavily striped black-and-cream painted walls. It's a very vital room in terms of both color and pattern.

Nuances of neutrals. Lacquered off-white walls, natural-textured upholstery, natural wood, natural leather, pre-Columbian sculpture in natural earth tones, a zebra rug, straw flowers combine textures to make a dramatic room in tones of only one color.

A New York brownstone. In this living room the mellow tones of brick, natural leather and beautifully polished floors are accented by a Dutch library cabinet in black.

The color of the islands. Natural straw on the walls—a neutral with texture—is mixed with the stark white of the ceramic fireplace and floor. The green upholstery duplicates the jungle greens beyond the windows. The accent color here is in the mellow natural leather that blends with the color of the beams.

Camel—a new neutral. Block foam upholstered in linen velvet contrasts in texture with the painted walls and the furniture, all of natural wood. Here, the accent color is in the off-white of paper lanterns designed by Isamu Noguchi.

The Non-Rules of Color

Choose the colors you want to live with, using as source material ideas from classical and modern art, ideas from store displays, and a clipping file of rooms you like.

Don't be afraid of color. Living with it can give you great pleasure. Don't play it safe and end up with a room that you'll find boring after a while. It is constantly being said that so-and-so is the new "in" color. There is no such thing as a fashion color. All colors are good if used properly.

For living rooms it is wisest to use a solid color on walls—one of the neutrals.

For more intimate and personal rooms you can let go with more intense color, give vent to your flair for pattern.

For the most part work with one background (neutral) color, one secondary color, and a third accent color used in decorative pillows, accessories, flowers—dried or fresh —and groupings of your treasured possessions.

Afterthought: Since there are no true rules about the use of color, you can't very well break them, can you?

part vi / lighting: the fifth dimension

By now you must be aware that I am very concerned with mood. Light is as important to mood as any other factor in our environment. Lighting can make you feel on top of the world or depressed. It can disturb or be a very calming influence. Bright light keeps you on your toes. Lights that are dimmed down to the rich, warm tones of candlelight are moody and marvelous.

But lighting has two functions: A mechanical one as well as a mood-making one.

Your first consideration in the use of light springs from the way you live, because light takes a little planning. Do you need special outlets, like a plug in the middle of the floor for a lamp that sits on a worktable in the center of the room as part of a furniture grouping? Do you have paintings that need to be lit? A piece of sculpture? A tapestry? These are purely mechanical considerations but they have to come early in your thinking.

In recent years the equipment available for home lighting has become quite sophisticated. Now industrial and theatrical lights have been adapted for home use. Using them effectively can bring a real sense of drama to your home. After all, a room has many aspects. Different things occur in it at different times. At one time someone may be sitting and reading there. Another time a room will be full of people for a party. Obviously, the lighting has to be different for such different activities.

Aside from candlelight, which has its own specific uses, and firelight, which is the ultimate in romance, there are only five types of lighting equipment to use in a home: Table lamps and floor lamps, uplights and downlights, spotlights and floodlights, light walls and light as architecture. Let's take them up one at a time.

19/lamps

Right off, let me go on record as saying that I dislike most lamps. And when I specify "most" I mean lamps that call attention to themselves by being too elaborate—the kind that scream at you because of aggressive color or design instead of quietly becoming part of the decoration of a room. I pursue this in considerable detail in Part VII, Accessories. A lamp announces itself because when it's lit it draws your eye to it. Let us consider table lamps first.

I feel that a table lamp should be no higher than about twenty-four inches, and of the simplest design. Though you'll find a more detailed description in Part VII, let me say now, there are a few designs that I consider good, and they are classic: Pot shapes, candlestick forms, and any of the Oriental vase shapes. There are a handful of vase shapes that have been used through the centuries in the Orient that work well in traditional or modern rooms—both from the standpoint of shape and color.

In addition to conventional lamps, there are modern lamps with a sculpted look. These have freed me from the worry of getting lamps that would line up properly in a room. Further, they fit the need for sculpture in a room. You need the various shapes and the play of shapes and textures against one another. Sculpture is a very easy way to get highs and lows in a room. Today there are lamps that have beautiful shapes, and they do another tricky thing: They provide light.

As to floor lamps. I don't mean the old-fashioned "bridge lamp." Here, again, there are splendid contemporary designs.

Modern table lamps, "sculpted" lamps and floor lamps can be used in the most contemporary rooms and even in the most traditional rooms, if they're used as accent lighting. Nearly every photograph in this book demonstrates how I like to combine modern and traditional lamps in the same room—even modern sculptural forms of lighting in traditional rooms.

In addition to lamps, there are marvelous lanterns designed by Isamu Noguchi. They have a special spot in my affection because not only do they give very subtle lighting but each is a work of art, created by one of the world's finest sculptors.

In passing, a word or two about chandeliers: If you're using one let it be a really good one that is worth hanging. One of the more obvious places for a chandelier is over a dining room table. But they can work in entrance halls, and—where there is a high ceiling—even in a bedroom. Scale is an important factor in hanging a chandelier. A dinky chandelier hanging over a large table is better left unhung. Almost without exception, I would say that if you think the chandelier you've chosen is the right size, it's probably too small. If you have a round dining table that is thirty-eight to forty inches in diameter, your chandelier could be thirty to thirty-six inches.

A chandelier should be hung low enough so that when you're seated at the table the bottom of the chandelier is just above your sightline—about at your hairline.

These are, of course, generalizations, because so much depends on the scale of the room, the scale and mood of the furniture, and the nature of the chandelier itself—some are light and delicate, others have bulk and heft. If you have any doubt, consult a professional.

20/uplights and downlights

Downlights

If a room is in any way in transition between modern and traditional, or if it is completely modern, the effect of a beautiful chrome downlight in the ceiling, where you would ordinarily have a chandelier, is lovely. Particularly in a dining room setting. There are two ways a downlight can be used: If you have a round table that is not too large, install a spotlight in the downlight fixture. This forms a beautiful pool of light, dramatizing a flower arrangement or whatever happens to be in the center of the table. I find this effect extraordinarily beautiful.

Of course, a spotlight is a concentrated circle of light that is very intense. You might want to use a downlight with a floodlight bulb. A floodlight comes down in a large cone shape with less intensity and illuminates a wider area of the table. But take care to judge the size of the bulb properly so that light doesn't shine in people's eyes.

For a longer, rectangular table you can have two or even three downlights, depending on the shape of the table. These can be equipped with either spotlight or floodlight bulbs depending on the lighting effect you want.

You can use a downlight in an entrance hall, or in an apartment where most of the rooms are off one corridor, you can have a series of downlights along the corridor.

I mention downlights right on the heels of chandeliers, because downlights can be installed in nearly every room where there is an outlet for a chandelier. If you are building a house or are doing extensive reconstruction you can have downlight outlets put wherever you want them—that is, if you have an idea what your room arrangement is going to be and where you will need them. If you're in an apartment or a house where outlets exist, you can easily install downlights. There are some beautiful swivel ones on the market that can be directed either against a wall or against a plant or against some element in a room you want to highlight.

Uplights

In recent years I have become more and more excited by the kind of room that has few or no lamps, a room illuminated with downlights and uplights. Particularly uplights.

These are canister lights—either round or square—in a great variety of diameters. Uplights can be set on the floor in the corners of rooms, at either end of a sofa, or behind plants and aimed toward the ceiling to give general illumination to a room. If your room is strictly for conversation and listening to music, where it's not essential to have a lamp to read or work by, you can create beautifully dramatic lighting with downlights and uplights.

Uplights can be bought almost anywhere. They come in many sizes to hold varying intensities of bulbs. They're portable. You can use them for accent light. Aimed at an enormous piece of sculpture, an uplight will project a beautiful shadow against the wall. I like to place uplights—one or two or three—on the floor behind plants not only to light the plants but to cast shadows upward on the walls and ceiling. You see, most furniture groups are rectangular. Suddenly you introduce the beautiful, free shape of a tree (palm, ficus, dracaena marginata) with a light shining up through it. It creates a contrasting mood with the massed furniture that would be very hard to achieve any other way.

Spotlights

In addition to uplights that sit on the floor, there are all manner of accent spotlights available. There are small spots that can be attached to the wall with a magnetic backplate and pointed in any direction you want. You could put such a spotlight on the side of a bookcase or another unobtrusive location and perhaps shine it against a grouping on a table, or on some object that needs to be accented or highlighted.

The whole contemporary technique of lighting is to create pools of light in a room regardless of whether it's done with table lamps or table lamps combined with uplights, or those extra little accent lights. The point is this: Don't have a room lit so that the level of all the lighting is the same. You should have general light, accent light, pools of light, and—here and there—little spots of light to pick up something you wish to call attention to.

Wallwashing

Another use of downlights is wallwashing. Let's say that you have a collection of paintings on a wall. It will be a knockout if you wash the paintings—in part or totally—in light from downlights above them, leaving the space between the paintings more dimly lit.

Track Lighting

This is a very effective way of achieving lighting versatility and doesn't require elaborate electrical work. The tracks come in polished chrome and many other materials, and are applied to the surface of the ceiling. On the track go spotlights that can be focused on anything in the room. The actual lights themselves can accommodate either spotlight or floodlight bulbs.

I have used track lighting in many ways: U-shaped, rectangles all around the ceiling, many other ways. I find a mixture of floodlight and spotlight bulbs works best. If I want to illuminate a general area I shine a floodlight on it. Then, from the opposite side of the track I might shoot a spotlight for another dimension of sharp focus within the softer illumination of the floodlit area.

In one of the model rooms I used a polished chrome ceiling track with square bullet spots. This is a very subtle, conservative, yet exciting form of lighting. The equipment is beautiful in itself, and it creates interest on the ceiling. (I don't think nearly enough is done with ceilings.) Further, ceiling spots give you wonderful opportunities to do things with the whole room. You can have a relatively blank wall with nothing much on it, but a pool of light or two from overhead track fixtures can make it a very commanding point of interest.

21/a light wall

Ideally, lights should be installed in the ceiling during construction. But that does require a little pre-planning so you know where you want fixtures for wallwashing, for floodlighting, for spotlights, and for pinpoint accent lights. Wherever possible—either during construction or when installing new lighting fixtures—put lights on dimmers so that the intensity of the light can be controlled.

In a modern room you can have either one whole wall or a divider wall composed of translucent plexiglass lighted from behind. Most plexiglass is available up to forty-eight inches wide without being specially ordered. You must then construct some sort of wood grid into which the plexiglass panels can be fitted so that they won't buckle. You can divide the wall into three, four, five, or as many spaces as you want, depending on its length. The most effective color of plexiglass is either white or off-white translucent. Your light wall should be about a foot away from the light units so that the illumination they project will diffuse evenly on the plexiglass.

If you have an ugly view or windows that are not particularly exciting, you could use a light wall in place of drapery and wall treatments. You might have sliding panels set in tracks at the floor and ceiling, like Japanese shoji screens. But the tracks would have to be substantial enough to support the plexiglass sheets. The screens could then be moved along the tracks to permit ventilation and access to the area behind them.

186

The Neil Simon Room. This room was an entertainment in itself because it was electronically programmed for ten light changes which ran in automatic order. In actual living conditions, these changes could be controlled manually to suit the mood of the occupants or could be set to change automatically. Light in its many aspects was the first thing to catch the eye. The background wall was constructed in twelve columns, divided by two-foot spaces of bronze plexiglass. The lighting effects were designed to show through and against this wall. The columns were hollow and contained shelves at various levels to hold sculpture, books and decorative accessories. At specified intervals these columns turned to face the viewer, timed with automatic lighting changes to bring the accessories into changes of focus —some intensely spotlighted, some backlit to create silhouettes, some illuminated in the soft, indirect glow of light through the bronze plexiglass of the structure. (These changes of display and light are ideal for anyone who has a lot of decorative accessories but doesn't want them all on display constantly.) In this room sculpture dominated sometimes, sometimes objets d'art. Sometimes the mood of light alone.

Light as architecture: In this room, which was really designed to be a *pied-à-terre* on a Greek island, the effect is white on white on white. In the foreground is white ceramic tile. The upholstery, the architecture, the walls —everything is white. Separating the area of living and dining from the conversation pit is a path of light that completely surrounds the furniture grouping. It's truly architectural light. It has a metal grid of polished steel over white plexiglass lit from below with fluorescent lighting. This is a very effective form of indirect lighting used in an unexpected area—the floor.

Wallwashers. You can see them used emphatically on the back wall, which was built-in and extended the length of the sofa. The bottom of the niche forms a ledge at the back of the sofa which serves as a display base for a collection of pre-Columbian sculpture. Wallwasher lights from above send down equal beams of light irregularly illuminating the wall. In the foreground is one of the sculptured lighting pieces I referred to. It gives enough light for anyone to work by, and is a splendid piece of sculpture when not in use. At the upper right is a floor lamp that bears no relationship whatsoever to the old-fashioned kind. It's wedged in between the ceiling and the floor, its enormous arm swinging out over the sofa to create a pool of light on the cocktail table.

Light as accessory. Here is one of the superb lantern sculptures of Isamu Noguchi. Not only does it set the dining room aglow with light, it becomes a major accessory in the room and sets a mood of charm-with-opulence even though the room is remarkably understated. By day this lamp acts as a unifying element for dining table and chairs. Lighted, it becomes as hypnotic as the moon.

Light as fantasy in a trellised room, complete with cupola. The entire room, though quite Edwardian in feeling, is brought up to date by backing the trellises with translucent white plexiglass and completely lighting them from behind. The effect is of several dimensions of light. There are table lamps—simple candlestick shapes with bouillotte shades made of steel to blend with the steel of the furniture. In this same area, there is a round plexiglass pedestal, lighted, which serves as a base for a Chinese vase and, in other parts of the room which do not show, other pedestals as bases for small plants. There are spotlights on the floor, shining up through the trees, throwing lacy shadows on the walls. This look of total lighting gives the room a very soft ambiance. It was a delight to be in it.

Light and beams. This room combines many of my favorite elements: Beams, which I have used over and over again in many different ways, and, instead of plaster between the beams, translucent white plexiglass lit from behind. The wood is unfinished cedar. When combined with the translucent look of white plexiglass it makes for a very dramatic room. Though the inspiration for it comes from eighteenth-century country architecture, light makes the room contemporary.

Wall projections. They're very complicated to do, but they can be extraordinarily dramatic. In this room I used see-through, blowup furniture in bright orange plastic. There were projections on the walls, on the ceiling, and on the floor. They were shot right through the plastic furniture. Here, you can see the projection of simple white columns on the white chairs. In all, there were about sixty different projections: Children playing ball in the park, tumbling waves, a beautiful pastoral scene with flowers and cows grazing. If you were using projections in your own home you could program fewer of them, or you could stop the projector at any place and have one scene for an entire evening. Or you could start out with a pastoral scene and switch to classical architecture, like the columns in this picture. (This slide was actually an old engraving demonstrating the principles of perspective.) Some of the slides were black and white, others were in color. In the color plate you can see the scuba divers in the underwater projection.

This is an avant-garde way to use light and to bring instant change to a room. But you need a knowledge of the principles of optics to create this effect. Some walls need a wide-angle lens in the projector, others a shorter lens. If you know someone who is informed about projections and the space necessary to make them work, try it.

Illuminated, architectural supergraphic. In the past years I've used painted supergraphics on the walls of a number of rooms, and I thought I'd go a step further and build them out into *architectural* supergraphics. Then I thought it would be fun to have light shoot up through them, and I added color so that a graphic would throw a glow through an entire room. The elements are three dimensional. Adding color lends a fourth. Light becomes the *fifth dimension*. It's all done with concealed fluorescent light that glows through the plexiglass. You'll see my favorite lighting technique —a light behind a palm tree projecting shadows on the wall.

Lampshades made from pebbles. The pebbles came from the beach, all smooth and shiny from the action of surf and sand, and all carefully selected for various shades of white. Then they were held together with solder to create a contemporary version of a Tiffany lamp. I love this kind of modern lighting.

Accent lighting. The great chandelier is composed of alternating spotlights and floodlights. These can be focused on various elements in the room to give accent highlighting as well as general illumination. If you look closely at the side of the desk you'll see a very simple form of floor lamp that gives enough light to make the desk usable as a work space. Yet, when the lamp is turned off it's unobtrusive. At the rear of the mirror-topped console table is a sculptural modern light which does nothing more than throw a closeup glow on a collection of very beautiful Japanese lacquer boxes —that's its only function in the room.

part VII/accessories: the final touches

No matter how much work and planning have gone into a room, I feel that the total look isn't complete until every last accessory is in place. I don't suggest that you have a rigid plan or arrangement in accessories. You'll change your mind as you go along; you'll find better places for objects; you'll move them for better balance; and obviously no one goes out and buys everything he needs for a room all at once.

Whenever I do a model room the procedure is the same—room after room, year after year. There is a time when the architecture is completed, the painters have done their work, the carpet is laid (if it's to have a wall-to-wall carpet). It might be pretty, but it's a bare room, nonetheless. The furniture goes in next, carefully and properly arranged for balance —a subject we have talked about in connection with furniture arrangement, and a subject that we still have a lot to say about. Because balance is important in a room, right down to the smallest final accessory.

The next most important thing is lighting. Lamplight, indirect lighting or spotlights—the overall light in a room is another dimension in decorating. I have already covered the subject of general lighting. Now I'd like to concentrate on lamps. They are an important part of room decoration, but I have found that this is one area where people go berserk. They use lamps that are wildly out of scale for a room, the wrong color, too garish. I am all for extreme simplicity in lamps. In the traditional vein my taste ranges from simple, classic lamps in brass, bronze or wood to porcelain or other ceramics. I particularly like candlestick lamps and pot shapes—from antique bean pots in all their natural pottery shapes to highly glazed contemporary versions. By pot shapes, I mean big, fat shapes that have some

mass. They fit best in today's decorating.

I feel very strongly that a lamp in traditional rooms should be either an authentic period lamp or a totally faithful reproduction of an old shape. Most good, old lamps in fine antique shops and even the good reproductions were not necessarily lamps to begin with. I have mentioned candlestick lamps. There are others, like Chinese vases, ginger jars and such. The simplicity of the forms make them perfect for lamps.

The placement of lamps in a room is very important for two reasons: They are a source of illumination for a room, and they are, in my mind, a major architectural element after furniture. A lamp and its shade are a block of shape in a room, and must be dealt with like any other mass. So they must be placed not only for light, but for room balance as well.

First of all function. Lamps create light— the fifth decorating dimension. In the section on lighting I have explained that, for me, it's important to have all lamps in a room the same height. This is for functional reasons of illumination as well as for balance.

Lamps and shades as decorative masses look better when all are on the same level. If I had my way in the design of a room I would have the heights of doorways and windows the same. For example, if you have a reasonably tall lamp on a lamp table (which is low) and, close by you have a console table or desk or writing table—all taller than the lamp table—you'll want a lower lamp on the desk, say, so that the lampshades will be at the same height. If your lamp in the sofa area is tall and skinny, then the lamp on the console table could be shorter and squatter for balance.

The key to decorating a room is in the

order of dominance of the elements. Biggest, big, smaller, smallest. I keep stressing the word balance because it is the one thing that makes the difference between a slapdash job of decorating and a professional one. For a professional, balance comes instinctively. I know that if I put something tall in this corner of the room, I need another tall thing in the opposite corner to balance it. Our eyes are trained that way. But non-professionals and even talented amateurs tend to forget balance, or don't pay enough attention to it right down to the smallest accessory.

After considering the balance of the mass of lamps in a room and the balance provided by the light of these lamps, there are other considerations. Like the balance of color.

As a general rule (which, like all rules, I break constantly when the occasion calls for it) I like to have lampshades all the same color and all the same style. Now, lampshades may vary in size to suit the lamps they're used on, but if you've got one lampshade with distinctly slanted sides, then I think all the lampshades in the room should have distinctly slanted sides.

There are three lampshade shapes that are my particular favorites. They are: The coolie shade, which is shaped like a Chinese coolie's hat, very slanted; the shade that is shallower and only slightly slanted called a bouillotte shade; and a deeper, moderately slanted shade called empire.

And there are only three colors that I use for lampshades in a living room: Black, dark espresso brown or white/off-white. In a bedroom wallpapered in some festive color, I might have lampshades in a bright yellow, a bright blue, or some gala color that works with the other colors in the room.

On traditional lamps I am inordinately fond of metal shades. These can be polished stainless steel (or aluminum that looks like it) or black tole shades, which are metal and painted with an antique finish.

While we're on the subject of color and texture, I feel that all the lamps in a room should be of the same material. For example, if you like brass lamps, every lamp in a room should be brass, not one brass, another marble, another plaster, etc. There are variations on this rule of similarity. If you're using porcelain lamps, one could be patterned in, say, two colors. Then you might have another porcelain lamp (or a pair of them) in a solid color that matches the predominant color of the patterned lamp.

I like to have a pair of matching lamps in a room, but not necessarily at either end of a sofa. My way of using a pair of lamps would be to place one at one end of a sofa and its partner somewhere else in the room at the same height. I might put one of a pair on a console table behind a sofa and the other across the room on a desk or a table. Then, if I wanted more light and another element of balance in the sofa grouping I would use another lamp that doesn't match, but bears a visual relation to the pair.

So far we have placed the biggest accessories—the lamps. There they sit casting lovely pools of light on the tables. Soon those illuminated areas will get filled in, but not yet. Next in the order of dominance come big pictures and mirrors.

I know we have already talked about big-scale paintings and mirrors. And though it gets repetitious, balance, again, is the keynote.

Let's say you have a white-walled room and a conversation grouping in the center of the floor dominated by an orange sofa. On the opposite side of the room might be a wooden console table or a commode or other storage piece. It would be very appropriate to hang a painting over it, which has either a touch of orange or in which orange is the predominant color.

Next step: You might have a space between two windows at the end of a room, or an off-center arrangement with a commode at the far end of your sofa. It makes sense, if you've already hung a great painting opposite the sofa, to hang a mirror or a pair of smaller paintings over the commode. Balance in a room must not only be from wall to wall but from corner to corner.

At this stage, you wouldn't want to hang every painting you own. I'm suggesting that you only place large, important paintings, again, in the order of dominance. We are beginning now what I call the build-up of accessories.

It may seem that we are bouncing from wall to wall, from corner to corner in this room we're putting together, but that's exactly the point. You work all parts of the room simultaneously, never just one area at a time. If you're going to hang that important painting at one end of the room, the other end of the room must have some element to balance it. Sometimes I have a very big accessory that I might put in at this point in the order of dominance—perhaps an impressive piece of sculpture on a cocktail table or in front of a mirror, if it seems the only likely spot for it. But, generally, the next thing I do in this build-up is to accessorize bookshelves or cabinets because bookshelves, armoires and étagères are usually the major items in a room.

I like to use lights in all bookshelf arrangements wherever possible. It's great if you have built-in lighting, but, if not, you can improvise. If you have an armoire with chicken wire backing the glass and want to do an interesting arrangement behind the wire, light is important. Since most cabinets do not come with built-in light, I usually put a small lamp in an armoire with a cluster of small accessories and then a whole lineup of books.

Books are very important to rooms—whether you have a great collection of art books or current novels or fine old leather-bound books. The mass of color that is suddenly injected into a room when you fill bookshelves is very exciting, particularly when you have a lot of them. The same would be true of any big collection. In terms of mass, it represents your next important element in the accessory build-up.

Now we come to those beautiful pools of light created by the lamps in your room—the next areas in the room to be accessorized. But with what? Let's consider what I think are beautiful accessories in a room.

My first advice would be: Put what you like in a room—on your shelves, tabletops, credenza. Put it there because you like it and it pleases you, not because it's what someone has suggested. Accessories give personality to a room. They should be the expression of **your** personality.

One decision you'll have to make is: Clutter or no. I have two attitudes. I like some rooms accessorized according to an almost Oriental point of view—a few beautiful, choice accessories, one exquisite bowl on a long console table. Or one attractive piece of sculpture. A truly lovely box. But if you are going to accessorize with Oriental restraint you have to have quite special possessions. For most people a delightful look can be achieved with the accumulation of objects, that are more personal than costly. Accumulations can be very attractive arranged in what might be called organized clutter.

22/collections

Collecting is great fun. I have always been a collector of the most widely divergent categories of stuff and nonsense. I have brought back objects from all the countries I've visited. I collect everything from wooden Japanese puzzles that fit together in the shape of animals and cost just a few pennies to French blue opaline. In between I have accumulated a vast collection of baskets and boxes of all sizes and types. I'm sure that everyone has a collection of something. If not, it's never too late to start, and when you accessorize a room you have a splendid opportunity to display the things you're fond of.

Boxes are near the top of my list of collectible things. I believe in boxes, from the tiniest little tortoise-shell or Battersea enamel boxes to enormous ones that can almost be chairside tables. This would include trunks that can be used as cocktail tables, or simply for the storage of toys or linens.

If your taste leans to the modern there are marble, alabaster, chrome, stainless steel or sterling silver boxes. For more traditional rooms there are boxes made of shells, snakeskin, precious woods. There are great steel boxes constructed with huge, elaborate locks —heavy because they were used as small safes and their great weight would discourage anyone from running off with them. There are boxes of malachite, lapis lazuli, glass, terra cotta. No matter what mood your room is in —from very traditional to spare contemporary, there are boxes of all kinds that you can use not only as decorative accessories but to hold things.

Boxes need not be expensive. Sometimes the least expensive is the one that has the most charm. Some years ago one of my assistants made a box for me. Just a plain, wooden box, completely upholstered in newspaper. It cost little—other than time and affection—and it's still one of my favorite possessions.

Bear in mind that in addition to looking attractive, boxes are terribly functional because of the myriad things we all have that need to be put away. On a cocktail table you can have a collection of boxes of various sizes that blend with one another to create a grouping. But one can hold cocktail napkins, another coasters, another playing cards. A box can hold a collection of nuts—for looking or eating.

When I say that boxes need not be expensive, I am thinking of all the places where every kind of accessory can be bought at reasonable prices. There are import shops that feature merchandise from all over the world at very nearly a "cost plus" basis. There you can find ceramics, baskets, boxes, candles, sculpture, dried flowers—many things that can reflect your taste yet are not costly. Most department stores offer any number of accessories in many departments—housewares, china, import shop, some even have special collections of accessory items to stimulate your imagination. You can usually find something that's within your budget—and, to repeat, you should allow room in your decorating budget for accessories.

I have a suggestion for a collection. From England come wonderful carved wooden objects called treen. They're almost always very small things—boxes, little goblets or chalices, miniature compotes. Some are in the shape of apples or pears, some are in splendid fruitwoods, always they are meticulously carved and finished. I admire the natural beauty and simplicity of treen and recommend it to you as something to collect.

Sculpture

Along with boxes, sculpture is on my list of favorite accessories. I find it indispensable in accessorizing because of the shape and excitement it brings to a room. Sculpture in any of its forms and in every medium: Primitive sculpture of Africa, Oceania, pre-Columbian, scrimshaw, Oriental sculpture from great temple figures to small ivory figurines. Small pieces of sculpture can be grouped together to give a cluster effect, and they're quite lovely standing all together on black teak stands.

Then there are all the variations in modern sculpture. There are kinetic compositions, with flashing light and internal movement, and plexiglass sculpture that can be lit from below or behind.

I don't know anyone who doesn't like sculpture of some kind. Fortunately today there are fine reproductions and even original works that are anything but costly.

Bowls

Next to sculpture and boxes, my favorite objects in a room are bowls. A deep bowl can hold flowers or cocktail nibbles. A really decorative bowl can stand alone or be a pretty complement to other elements in an accessory grouping. A shallow bowl can be used as an ashtray. Like boxes, bowls come in all manner of materials, from the crudest pottery to high lacquer bowls from the Orient. Generally, I like ceramic bowls, be they crude or highly sophisticated, because of the particular texture they bring to a room.

Along with bowls, ashtrays are important, both to round out an accessory grouping and to be functional for those who smoke. But I mean ashtrays with authority, not tiny little ones.

In a traditional setting a lovely dessert or salad plate could serve as an ashtray—or the survivor of a broken set of bread and butter plates could go on a small table. But no matter what its origins, an ashtray should be large enough to hold a cigarette without its rolling off.

In contemporary settings I like large important-looking ashtrays made of beautifully shaped ceramic, chrome or stainless steel. By shape, I don't mean free-form, amoeba shape. I mean either round or rectangular ashtrays with a well-designed profile, made of superb materials.

Clocks

I happen to be fond of clocks and think they are important accessories. Grandfather clocks are more than timepieces. They're perfect to balance a large architectural element or piece of furniture in another part of the room. My preference is for grandfather clocks that are fairly simple and country-looking rather than the more elaborately carved and constructed types.

There are as many types and styles of clocks as there are materials to make them. And all sizes as well. Clocks also make great collections. Of course they are functional, but they also have interesting shapes and textures to be incorporated into accessory arrangements.

Boxes, bowls, sculpture, clocks—these are just some of the many, many kinds of accessories you can use in a room. If you begin to think of the things you have, the things you collect, the things you would like to have, there are more than enough for you to use as accessories. But let me repeat: Show off the things you have and love. Don't use something as an accessory just because someone told you to.

23/the build-up

Before we go about placing accessories in a room, let me say something about grouping. Accessories must be selected and assembled with the casual exactness of a painter arranging a still life. Their textures and shapes should be compatible. Too many things are tiny, and are meaningless by themselves or scattered around a room. If you have a collection of small things like snuff boxes, then group them all together. Don't spread them around. If you love your collection, cluster it all together and light it so that it shows to its best advantage for others to enjoy as well. In most cases three to five items are enough for a grouping on a table or mantelpiece—but this isn't inflexible.

Tabletop Arrangements

Let's return to that pool of light gleaming down from a lamp on a table. Depending on the height of the lamp, it would be lovely to have either a live green plant, a bouquet of flowers, or a basket filled with some kind of straw flowers filling in the bulk of the area between the tabletop and the bottom of the lampshade.

This forms a background for the rest of the accessories you place in the grouping. In front of flowers or plants, you might group a cluster of small pieces of sculpture or one bigger piece of primitive art. The height of this additional element or group might be half the distance between tabletop and the bottom of the lampshade. We are thus constructing a visual arrangement much like a lopsided pyramid. The lamp is your tallest element. Then you fill in the area between lamp and table from the tallest secondary element to the lowest point, which could be an ashtray or a fairly flat box. The elements used to achieve this pyramid effect might be a combination of wood, metal, porcelain and flowers. Try to keep the textures varied. If you have something shiny, like porcelain, then contrast it with something that is rather "dry" in texture. Contrast shapes as well. If you have something that is bulky, balance it with something fairly tall and slender. Variety is an important factor in balance.

We return to our key word again: Balance. Not only is it important in the overall arrangement of the room, but within each and every element of a room. Balance is the secret to the composition of every fine still life you've ever seen. It's also the secret of composing a still life of accessories on a tabletop.

Other elements that you could use for building up the space in a pool of light might be a stack of boxes with similar styling. Or a small painting on an easel. For a more modern look you could take one of the splendid modern frames available today and fill it with a collage you have done yourself, or a painting or drawing by a member of your family.

A cocktail table presents a different set of considerations. On a cocktail table I believe in big, tall, important pieces. Don't forget, you've got this low table down in the valley between chairs and major upholstery so it has to have something placed on it that enables it to stand up against and balance the bulk of all the surrounding pieces. Another

reason I like something big on a cocktail table is to have an attractive and dramatic center of interest in the room.

One cocktail table combination could be a piece of sculpture, a box and a big ashtray. Don't cover every inch of horizontal space, however. You need room to set down a drink, or to put a tray of food or a coffee service. Leave room for these more functional uses of a cocktail table.

Balancing the Room

Achieving balance within a group of accessories is not enough. That group has to be balanced in turn by other elements in the room. An example: You have a lamp table at one end of a sofa with a grouping of accessories on it. Further, there is a console table behind the sofa. The bulk of your accessory arrangement on the console table should be at the end *opposite* the lamp table. Let us further assume that the group on the lamp table is indeed built around a lamp, and you are not using a lamp on the console table. Then the accessory build-up on the console table should balance the height and the bulk of the grouping beside the sofa.

Let us go one step further. If you have a grouping on the console table and on the lamp table, it becomes even more important to have something on the cocktail table to add a third point of balance—a tall sculpture, a vase filled with green leaves, pampas grass—something to bring height to the cocktail table. You might use a big plant with a downlight overhead (with a spotlight bulb in it) to drench the plant in light. This is not only good for the plant, it's another touch of light— the fifth dimension.

205

Plants

Let's consider what to do with an area of the room that needs something tall and big. Say there are high windows. In another part of the room you have a section of wall that needs something to balance an armoire or étagère across the way. There is absolutely no need or reason to add another piece of furniture. That's the place for a plant. A plant can break up the bareness of the wall and lend a tall, big shape for balance. By plant, I mean a *tree*—a big palm tree or a ficus or dracaena marginata. Something big that goes from floor to ceiling, placed in a pot that fits with the look of the room—decorative terra cotta, stainless steel, or plain white stoneware. This tall, leafy plant helps to balance the weight of the massive pieces of furniture and the soft edges of the plant act as a contrast to the hard edges of the wooden pieces—particularly when an uplight throws shadows on wall and ceiling.

There might be a little spot on the wall between the spread of the palm leaves. That's a good place for a colorful little painting to peek through the leafy green.

Plants other than potted trees that can be used effectively in accessory arrangements are asparagus sprengeri (also known as asparagus fern), piggybacks, most ivy including grape ivy, even cactus. The plants you use in a room depend on the amount of light the room gets, and the geographic area you live in. In some instances cactus is appropriate because some are big and bold enough to give you a large sculptural shape for balance.

Usually I use only one kind of large plant in a room. For instance, if I'm using palms, every plant in the room is a palm. I am pleased by the effect of three trees of one kind in one room—either bunched together, or spread through the room as elements for balance.

I am of two opinions about flower arrangements. They depend on the nature of the room—although I firmly believe that every room can do with flowers. In most instances I like masses of one kind of flower in a room—all of the same color. On the other hand, in a country room that is more rustic in feeling, I think very ordinary field flowers in a grand mix of colors and textures are exactly right.

The Final Balances

At this stage of accessorizing it's time to take a look around and achieve the final balances. Is there an empty spot somewhere? I don't mean that every inch of the room must be filled up, but is there an empty spot that needs weight to offset a heavy element somewhere else in the room? I like to hang and place things in unorthodox places. I'm prompted to do this by an eye that has been trained over the years to watch out for balance. Usually, if I get an urge to place something in a surprising spot, it's because my subconscious has told me that it's needed for balance—not necessarily for surprise. You may have to look around your nearly completed room and carefully analyze the groupings. Then you may decide that you want a standing cluster of accessories on the floor, and you could put a miniature chest of drawers or a trunk or a big stack of art books next to a chair—something that has bulk and can also provide a surface to set something on.

You may not be able to accessorize a room totally in one session. You may want to look around for a day or two and make changes and adjustments. The more you practice and change the more your eye will become attuned to balance of mass, texture and weight. And remember, your accessorizing isn't permanent. You'll want to change it. And you should.

I have to change the model rooms constantly because things are sold out of them. They may be kept intact for the first week, but sooner or later nearly every accessory is sold and I have to replace them. Sometimes I do it bit by bit, sometimes it's done in one fell swoop. Change can be refreshing, because it forces you to take a completely new look at the room.

Just as it isn't necessary to put every accessory you own on display, it's not necessary to arrange the room and then "freeze" it for all time so that a visitor today and five years from now would see the same accessories. Keep some of your things in hiding. Then, once in a while, you can bring out a few and create an entirely new still life to replace an old one. The day you buy a bunch of new spring daffodils it might be a happy idea to bring out a yellow Ming vase to put them in. There should always be the opportunity—and the materials—for a certain amount of impromptu replacement of accessories. I have said that rooms serve many purposes and have many moods—from private to party. Just as you should be able to change the lighting and even the furniture arrangement from time to time, so you should be able to alter the arrangement of your accessories.

Let me do a quick recap of the stages of accessorizing:

1. After basic units of furniture are arranged for balance among themselves and in relation to architectural features, place your lamps for equal height and the distribution of weight and mass in the room.

2. Where each table lamp spills a pool of light arrange accessories in a lopsided pyramid to fill in the spaces between tabletop and lampshade bottom.

3. Balance one still life of accessories in one area of the room with another arrangement in another area.

4. As you go through the build-up of accessories, always be on the lookout for balance among the various points of interest in the room. Be aware of heights as well as masses. Use large pieces of sculpture to fill a space that wants a point of interest. Use big trees to balance door openings or high windows. Be on the lookout for a spot on the wall that wants color or mass.

5. In general, look at your room two ways: As in the floor plan, view it straight down for furniture and architectural balance; and consider its horizontal perspective to determine if the graph—the ups and downs—created by the many layers of accessories is balanced for mass, color, texture and interest.

That one word: Balance. If you make every effort, you'll know you've achieved it when you feel at ease in the room, and feel that it is quite personally, quite specifically, *yours*.

This shows how an indoor tree can serve to enhance space. The area next to the credenza would be all right left as it is, but placing a plant there makes the area so much prettier. The soft lines of the plant not only lend a happy contrast to the hard-line architecture and furniture, but it's always surprising to see a tree indoors. On the right you'll see a little painting tucked low on the wall behind the tree. If you were stretched out on the chaise longue that painting would be a small colorful diversion right at your eye level.

The accessories here are all natural, and nature knows no period—it goes with everything, from traditional to extremely modern. Too, these natural things, like ostrich eggs, antlers, horns of all kinds, have naturally neutral colors that blend well with raw woods. Although the accessories are in great profusion, the look is natural.

208

The oversize piece of African sculpture on the large cocktail table is balanced by a large box of polished chrome—the arrangement completed by a small bush on the floor adjacent to the cocktail table. The painting on the wall lifts the eye up to give the effect of balance with the very strong architectural dominance of the plastic over the fireplace. Note the three wallwashers that illuminate the gems and minerals on the shelves.

This is one way to use accessories to balance a major piece of furniture. The armoire (with clusters of accessories lighted from the inside) is balanced by the grouping of the accessories on the credenza to the right. The gigantic scale almost equals the armoire in height. On the lower levels the accessories are smaller—the bouquet of baby's breath resting in the scale nearly fills in the space from the credenza to the bottom of the lampshade. You'll see that the thinness of the shaft of the scale is balanced neatly by the bulk and projection of the animal head mounted nearby on the wall.

This is my favorite accessory photograph. The fruit painting was part of a series of murals especially painted for this room and based on an antique Spanish painting, which is in my own collection. The large garden figure is terra cotta and sits on a red-painted Louis XV country buffet along with a still life of real fruit on a copper tray which repeats the fruit in the painting. I am very fond of the way the textures, shapes and colors in this grouping enhance each other. I call your attention to the spotlight on the wall giving a highlight to the figure, but leaving the mural to rest in the shadows behind.

I continually mention my predilection for placing large pieces of sculpture on a cocktail table, and here is an example. In a room that is predominantly black—walls, carpeting, lacquered furniture—this gilded Thai figure was very impressive and gave a strong accent point to the room. Along with it, a large Indian brass pot for a warm metallic accent contrasting with the glint of the polished chrome of the light wall behind the grouping and the contemporary ashtray.

211

Here is an elaborate conglomeration of accessories on a graceful black lacquer Louis XV desk with ormolu mounts. Even though the accessories are hodgepodge they blend nicely. On the left edge of the photograph you'll see the brass shade of a floor lamp which acts as the illumination for this work area.

Gathered in front of the exquisitely carved old Indian temple figure is an array of tiny tortoise-shell snuff boxes. Mixed with them is a globe lamp on a dimmer which forms a suitable and subtle lighting for this area—modern though it is. Here is a vast mix of mood and period: A Louis XV commode, Indian statuary, English tortoise-shell boxes, a contemporary light source and a pair of tusks in silver mounts—all against a Venetian mirror. And yet the mix works.

This illustrates accessories coming down the scale in order of importance. You will see a difference in scale and balance of accessories from the console tables on the left to the accessories on the cocktail table. In spite of the quantity of accessories there is still room enough on the cocktail table to place a tray of drinks or food. Because of the expanse of space, I used three cocktail tables together leaving a little space between them. The idea of combining them must have communicated itself, for people who bought the tables bought them in groups of three.

This picture demonstrates how a period mix can work in accessorizing. Here is an Empire bed with a red fox fur throw, an Empire commode with a collection of boxes and the most ornate Venetian tortoise-shell mirror above it—all used against a cinnamon brown woolen wall covering. Then, thrown into the mix, a modern graphics arrangement that balances the height of a window opposite (not shown in the photograph). These graphics give a grace note of lightness and brightness to an otherwise fairly subdued and traditional room.

Superclutter

In a traditional kitchen of seventeenth-century Spain are handmade tiles painted in authentic designs from a source in the area near Valencia. The accessories on the shelves include all the different size pitchers and pottery that you might have found in such a kitchen. An interesting architectural addition—the indoor well, always a part of any kitchen of the time.

This is a replica of a typical Japanese kitchen. In the foreground, the charcoal stove with rice boilers bubbling and steaming away over the coals. The Japanese cook more rice than they need at one time and then store the cooked rice in the wooden buckets seen on the top shelves at the right of the photograph. All of the implements you see here are authentic. On the left is a very stark, slate-lined indoor well.

Light as Sculpture

The simple modern lamp on the dining-worktable has an interesting sculptural shape. The plants are asparagus sprengeri (asparagus fern). Grouped together in this light, airy room, the lightness of the fern is exactly the right texture and the right color to go with the brightly colored Italian pottery.

Lighting here is architectural as well as sculptural. The cocktail table in the pit is a white plexiglass cube lighted from inside. The only lamp in the entire setting, on the ledge to the left, is a column of chrome with a half-round chrome shade. The wall in the background is plexiglass, too, lighted from behind. There are three different kinds of light in this room dominated by the orange, navy blue and white tile forming the surround. The storage wall of white and orange modular units conceals a spotlight that throws its beam to form a pool of light on the white fur pillow.

The enormous globe on a white enameled snakelike stand illuminates the whole corner of this room, but also stands as a compelling piece of sculpture—reflected many times in the mirrored corner, which serves to double the space of a relatively small room. At the end of the sectional unit upholstered in white leather is a round column, which acts not only as a pedestal for a lamp, but as a column of light in itself. On the ledge, mixed with a collection of pottery, is another lamp with a strong sculptural quality which blends beautifully with the shapes surrounding it and also gives an accent of light. Asparagus fern again.

The raised platform on the left is a light structure in itself. Orange plexiglass squares lighted from below form the floor. Standing on it are other forms of accessories—three triangular white plexiglass pedestals, one the base for a lamp. Here, I have broken the rule of all lamps on the same level, using this mushroom-shaped lamp as a piece of sculpture and getting it up in the air more as an accessory than as a source of light. In this room the accessories have been used in a very sparse way, with the exception of the étagère, where there is a collection of plexiglass blocks clustered together with a spotlight illuminating them and casting the shadows of all the objects onto the wall. Another touch of light: A collection of crystal teardrops filled with water and hung at varying heights to spill glitter into the room.

This picture illustrates the bulky look of the pot lamp—its light standing out against the dark leather of the books. The basket filled with dried flowers contrasts with the smoothness of the pot shape and fills in the space from the bottom of the lampshade to the tabletop. In this grouping there is room for only one ashtray, but it's a spectacular piece of porcelain. Here I grouped a collection of accessories on the cocktail table in various heights to balance the bulk of the sofa.

This room is fundamentally traditional, but has quite contemporary lamps of thin-stem chrome with half-round chrome shades. Here the lamp is definitely an architectural element that lends shine to the room as well as light. Withal, it's still not too austere in an otherwise traditional room. One lamp on the table is perfectly balanced by the floor lamp on the opposite side of the room, where it isn't necessary to have a lamp table.

On the lamp table next to the chair is a tall wooden candlestick lamp with a bouillotte shade. On the desk behind the sofa is a shorter wooden candlestick lamp balancing the height of the lamp on the table. I must mention the moldings in this room because they are truly remarkable, even though they have nothing to do with accessories. These moldings tie the whole room together visually —even enclosing a beautiful corner of books.

Lamps as accessories. Here are a group of Chinese vases, in a color known as *sang de boeuf*, some of which have been made into lamps and topped with ivory-colored shades. Thus, their main effect is that of accessories. Here, too, is an unusual use of plants. On the left is a live birch tree. It was brought into the room from the woods in all its winter bareness and put in water. After a while small green leaves appeared. It's a startling trick to use if you have access to live birch trees. I broke one of my own rules of all-of-one-kind plants and used cactus in the room because it was intended to be a desert retreat.

There are many other accessory and architectural points of interest in this room: The shine of the metal pedestals as accessories, the *sang de boeuf* vases and lamps mixed with Indian carvings, the glitter of the track lights on the ceiling, the ceiling itself of unfinished ash forming concentric squares separated by the track lights set flush with it. This is one way to use track light—to form theatrical pools of light to accent furniture groupings and accessories.

The allover shining touch. The shine is provided by a combination of many things: Bronze plexiglass covering everything—walls and floors. Further shine is lent by a deep-bronze glass cocktail table and dining table. The base of the cocktail table is polished chrome and that of the dining table clear plexiglass. The chairs in the dining area are of French polished steel. This is ultimate shine in a room. Note the highs and lows of the accessories grouped on the cocktail table—plants, sculpture, bowls and books.

Metal and crystal shine. On the glass cocktail table are clustered many forms of crystal —obelisk and prism shapes. Over it is an authoritative lamp in polished chrome. On the worktable is the chrome column lamp with matching half-round shade, and in the étagère still more accessories with a metallic glint. One sidelight: I'm particularly fond of the dark brown plush modular units that surround the cocktail table. This is only one of many ways to arrange these beautifully versatile seating units.

Glint of brass. In this case it's Moroccan brass. All of those rounded boxes you see on the desk and in the *armario* (Spanish translation of the armoire) and on the commode are betel nut boxes. They come in a raft of different shapes. They're used as sharp contrast to the jars and bowls in traditional blue-and-white pottery. I mentioned using an old safe as an accessory, and here it is, supporting a tall brass candlestick lamp whose height balances the shorter, similarly designed brass column lamp on the Portuguese desk.

part VIII / where to go for help

24/shopping your department store

There are a few things you should do in the way of preparation before you actually start buying for your home.

Do lots of thinking. Do lots of looking. Do lots of analyzing.

Be prepared with some idea of what you need and want for your home. When actually shopping, take along color samples, which you have accumulated from research, clipping and previous preliminary shopping. If your color scheme is fairly well thought out in advance you can avoid a lot of confusion and indecision.

Now, let's assume that you have your ideas fairly together and some sort of floor plan worked out. You'll probably be shopping in two stages. First, there's the shopping you do just to look, see what's available, and sort out your ideas. A department store is a logical place to shop because most fine stores are not only leaders in styles and trends, and have a great variety of things available—in fact almost everything a home could need—they also stand behind the merchandise they sell, and generally have a reputation for quality and reliability.

Too, most fine department stores have ex-perienced sales personnel in the various divisions, as well as a professional design and decorating staff that can give you anything from a few helpful suggestions to a complete design job.

Let me give you a few suggestions about what to look for when buying upholstered pieces, wooden furniture and bedding (that's the proper term for mattresses and springs or convertible sleep sofas—too frequently "bedding" is thought to mean sheets, blankets and pillows) because these are the items that seem to be cloaked in mystery, and the ones that most consumers tend not to understand. Let's take them one at a time.

What to Look for in Upholstered Pieces

Styling is the most obvious thing in large upholstered pieces because that's what's most evident. But let's not linger too long on the subject, because styling depends a great deal on the sort of room you're doing. In the furniture department of almost every fine store you'll find a tremendous selection of styles from totally traditional to ultra contemporary. What we're addressing ourselves to at this juncture is price and quality in furniture.

In budgeting the expense of upholstered pieces, you must consider whether the purchase is for long or short term. Is the piece you're considering something for the main room in your home? Is it something that's going to take a beating in the family room? If so, you need really strong construction and a fabric that is sturdy. Will you be apt to replace the piece after a few years? In other words, does your purchase have to last only until "we can afford a better sofa"?

227

You Get What You Pay For

In the matter of sofas or other large upholstered pieces, you can buy one for $400, for $1,200, even more. The price you pay depends on the details of the workmanship and the quality of the materials that go into it. It's a fairly reliable rule of thumb that when it comes to buying upholstered pieces *you get what you pay for.*

Most of what you're paying for is invisible—the frame, the filling, the springs. The tailoring and fabric are visible and feel-able, and you get an idea as to their quality. But you can't rip a sofa apart to see how it's made (even if you were expert enough to recognize quality) so price is about the only criterion you have.

Take the frame, for example. The kind of wood that's used to make it is very important. In an inexpensive sofa, you might get a light, soft wood that isn't properly dried. In one that costs more you might get the finest hardwood, which gives the sofa great stability and a long life.

It seems obvious, but another way to determine the quality of an upholstered piece is, simply, to sit on it. Sit in various positions, squirm a little. That way you'll get a fundamental feeling about the comfort of the furniture. There are considerations of scale, too, because a sofa that is comfortable for a long-legged man would not be so for a petite woman.

You have a choice of fillings in upholstered pieces. In general, there are three categories, with a wide range of possible combinations in between. There are many synthetic or man-made fibers that are used for furniture filling, all of which have brand names. If you have any doubt, ask. And look. And sit. And take the advice of the trained personnel in a reputable store.

Furniture with a specific filling may be on the floor as a sample. Perhaps a sofa will be shown with a feather and down filling, another with a polyester cushion wrapped in foam, still another in all foam rubber. It doesn't mean that the sofa you want can't have any of these fillings. Once again, ask.

The most luxurious look and the deepest comfort comes from a filling which combines feathers and down. You can have all down, or mostly down with few feathers, or lots of feathers and little down. One thing you might take into consideration is that any time anyone gets up you have to plump the cushions if they are filled with feathers and down. I don't mind this mild exercise. It's worth it for the luxurious feel and look you get.

But you can still have a luxury filling without plumping cushions. A soft plushy look can be achieved with foam wrapped in polyester, which gives cushions a luxurious crown. They look as if they had just been plumped. But when you sit and get up again the natural resiliency of this filling pops the cushions back to their original shape without any help from you. There are various degrees of quality in this type of filling, price being the determining factor.

Your third choice of filling is foam rubber. This gives you a very trim, tailored look and would be suitable for certain rooms. Take very modern, tailored foam covered with stretch fabric; some modular seating pieces are done this way, and though they look stiff—they're meant to—they're still comfortable when you sit on them.

These are general remarks, but they will serve to give you some idea of what questions to ask your store or dealer. And do ask. The men who sell furniture at any fine store are experts in their field and are happy to discuss furniture quality and construction with you. They're looking for customer satisfaction as much as you are.

I have found that a lot of people think that the very piece of furniture they see on the floor is the piece that they're going to get. This isn't true—at least, in most fine stores. Floor samples are for you to look at. Often they're incorporated into an overall display or color scheme—maybe a seasonal display. The piece you purchase can usually be ordered in other styles, sizes or upholstery fabrics than the floor sample.

Sofas come in a variety of standard sizes. You might look at a piece of furniture on the floor that is ninety inches long, and say, "Oh, I love the styling of that sofa, but it's just too long." Ask. Usually you'll discover that the sofa is available in a variety of sizes. 54", 60", 72", 80", 84" and 90" are all standard sizes; and, depending on the manufacturer and the price range, you can have that particular sofa in almost any size you want.

You also have a great selection of fabrics. It's important that you give some thought to the kind of fabric that you're interested in—color, pattern, texture. When you get to the store you should have a fair idea of what you want, because you're going to be presented with hundreds of fabrics to choose from. Do you want velvet or linen or heavy cotton? Do you want a solid color or a print? If you don't have some idea, the experience of choosing a fabric can be bewildering.

First, there are racks of fabric that the manufacturer has put together for you to select from. These are graded according to price, and the selection is usually considerable. In addition, it's possible to choose from a selection of "decorator fabrics" and decorating consultants are usually at hand to help you and your salesman.

Also on the subject of fabric: You can ask to have your fabric treated so that it repels soil and spills. There are several trade names for this process, and at a very small additional cost above the original price of the fabric one of these synthetic coatings can be applied. I really advise it. No matter how careful you are, there's always the possibility of a mishap, and certainly there's bound to be just everyday dust and soiling. It pays to protect fabric, particularly if you're buying good quality.

Another tip on buying fabric: Let's say that you're buying a sofa now but are postponing the purchase of two chairs or another major piece of upholstery until a later date. Then, I certainly recommend that you place an order for enough fabric to cover the future upholstery pieces as well as the sofa. This assures you of an exact color match because the fabric will all be from the same dye lot. One of the reasons why so many rooms are a mishmash of color is, I believe, because people buy things one at a time. Color is important, and I feel that color matches should be exact, not just close.

These bits of advice are nothing more than the basic clues to make buying furniture less complex for you. There are nuances upon nuances available to you if you're working with a professional designer.

What to Look for in Wooden Furniture

Construction is one of the first things you should look for. Is the piece you're buying well put together? Usually your eye will tell you, for well-constructed furniture has a substantial look to it. You can always lean on it to make sure it doesn't wobble.

Finish is another clue to quality. Is there depth and clarity to the finish? Does it look as though effort has gone into a really fine finish with the wood graining showing through? Or does the finish seem totally opaque, covered by the contents of a spray can?

In storage pieces you can examine the drawers. Are they properly dovetailed at the corners? Are the drawers finished on the inside? Are they smooth, so that the clothing you put into them won't snag? Is the hardware of good quality? (A little bit of looking will train your eye to begin to recognize the difference between good and shoddy hardware.) Are the drawers on runners so that they slide toward and away from you easily without sticking?

A good piece of wooden furniture has a well-constructed back; inexpensive furniture does not. Inexpensive furniture is perfectly acceptable for an extra room that doesn't get a good deal of use. Such furniture can even have a composition or heavy cardboard back.

Determining good styling requires a somewhat more expert eye. I am an enthusiastic exponent of traditional furniture that is authentically traditional and truly reflects the mood of the original antique that inspired it. If the piece you're considering is supposed to be in the period of Louis XVI, then it should be all Louis XVI, not with a lot of other period details thrown in. You can help yourself to understand style by doing a little research in books, magazines and good antique shops.

When it comes to modern pieces, I look for boxes. Simple, well-constructed boxes, untrimmed, in lavishly grained wood with a very clear finish, straight, uncluttered lines and very little extra adornment, only some metal trim perhaps in chrome (polished or brushed) and very simple hardware.

Completely opposite in feeling but equally appealing to me is wide modern furniture with half-round edges where normally there would be sharp edges. This works well with the molded look in upholstery. For me, modern furniture is pure architecture and should look it. Traditional furniture is, by comparison, architecture plus adornment.

In modern furniture I like either of two finishes: A richly grained wood in clear finish or lacquer that glistens like the finish on a fine automobile. For a lacquer finish you could buy a piece that is custom done in the ancient Japanese manner, which requires layers and layers of lacquer with hand rubbing in between. This is an absolutely breathtaking finish, but then so is the price. Fortunately, today there are excellent synthetic lacquer finishes that give a high degree of luster as well as a protective surface to furniture that gets considerable use.

A word about mass-produced furniture. The word "mass" no longer means "cheap," as it once did. We live in an age of highly sophisticated mechanization where it's possible to turn out pieces that are quite detailed at modest prices because techniques of manufacturing are improving every year (the same is true of finishing techniques).

Years ago any heavily carved or detailed piece of furniture had to be done by hand, which made it costly. Today there are multiple machines that can duplicate a hand-carved master sample for many, many pieces of furniture. Such machines might turn out twenty-four to forty-eight legs at a time. So that even the most elaborate details on French, Italian and Spanish furniture can be manufactured at a price that does not relate to the price of hand carving in any way.

What to Look for in Bedding

There is a parallel between buying shoes and buying bedding. Don't skimp on price. You'll only be uncomfortable. And you won't get the wear that you'd get from a more expensive purchase. It's very important that a bed fits your needs, just as shoes must fit your feet.

All stores have bedding in a complete range, from inexpensive to high priced, and each has its purpose. But the mattress that you sleep on nightly should be the very best. The very best costs only a few pennies a night more than an inexpensive mattress, so why not invest those few pennies in comfort and rest.

Some people think that because a child or teenager doesn't weigh much a good mattress is not necessary. Not so. They still need the support that a well-made mattress gives.

There are places, certainly, for less expensive bedding, such as a beach house, or a place where it's not slept on regularly. If the bedding is in a guest room, it can be of lesser quality because it isn't used every night.

Feel perfectly free to do what you're expected to do when shopping for a mattress. Lie down on it. Test it for comfort and firmness.

There is a very distinct advantage in a more expensive mattress. It retains its comfort and firmness for a longer time. That's because it's built of better materials in the first place.

Let me caution you not to consider a mattress by itself. A mattress and matching box spring are an inseparable team. If you've decided your mattress is worn out and you need new bedding, pitch out the whole thing and get a new mattress *and* box spring. They're engineered to go together. You may, for one reason or another, decide to switch to a foam mattress. The box spring that you have might not necessarily be structured to hold it. Always buy a set, even though it costs a little more. After all, your sleep is at stake.

When shopping for bedding, sit on the edge of the bed. Does it support your weight without bending a great deal? Part of the support it gives you comes from the framework that is used in the box spring. If you're buying a quality set, good wood will have gone into the frame and it will not only support your weight well but for a long time.

One other thing: If a bed is to be slept on by two people, it should support each person individually. A good bed is made in such a way that the sleeping surface is divided. It's firmer in the center so that the two occupants won't roll together.

To repeat myself, the foregoing is just to start you thinking and alert you to some of the things you should investigate when shopping for furniture. And to give you an idea of what questions to ask. And ask! Not only is it expected, the experts at a good store are more than happy to answer your questions. They are, after all, professionals in their field, and you should take advantage of their expertise.

25/ how does bloomingdale's do it?

For years now Bloomingdale's model rooms have served as a showcase for furniture and accessories from all over the world. But unless you are involved in the department store business, you might not realize the tremendous amount of time and effort that goes into these rooms. We've done a staggering amount of research in this country and all around the world. We have gone to provincial museums, combed old bookstores, libraries and archives, searched through antique shops, explored remote hamlets and generally steeped ourselves in the background material necessary to make and create a selection of furniture, fabrics, rugs and accessories. Then, after years of innovative buying and selling—suddenly we were aware of a lack.

Most of the furniture manufacturers in this country (with the exception of some fine cabinetmakers whose work was limited and costly) were using mass-production techniques with varying degrees of success. The kinds of home furnishings that were readily available to us in Europe, though appropriate to European living, were in no way related to what we were doing and how we were living in this country.

At that time, too, there seemed to be a growing interest in reproductions of antiques on the part of people who couldn't afford genuine ones but wanted to have good, authentic copies—not just adaptations. So we decided to present reproductions of antique pieces of furniture that fitted in with today's living. Thus was born our furniture import program.

To launch it took an enormous amount of time and travel. We would research and research before we made any choices. Once we had decided on a piece of furniture, we had it precisely reproduced with only minor changes of detail or scale. I mentioned villages and provincial museums earlier, mainly because their furniture was appealing and much more adaptable to life in the United States. The furniture and designs from places like Fontainebleau or Versailles were beyond the scope of a department store and certainly far too grand for most American homes.

The program has grown mightily since its beginnings. Today we work in most of the countries of Europe—Spain, Portugal, England, France, Italy, Scandinavia. We don't, as one might think, go to a showroom in a big European city and say, "I'll take three of those and five of those and ten of that." Here's how we work!

We go to small European manufacturers who do all or most of their work by hand. We spend hours over each piece of furniture, doing full-scale drawings, indicating every little detail of carving, hardware, interiors of drawers, color of leather, proportion. We work around the clock. It's not unusual for us to be at a factory at midnight or into the early morning hours working with a manufacturer on detail. Then we give these craftsmen time to make a sample of the furniture to show us when we go back a few months later. At that point we can make any necessary corrections.

The same method applies to accessories like lamps. We go right to a potter and work with him. He might turn a shape for us on the wheel to give an indication of what we could work with. Or we might bring a full-scale drawing of a lamp and wait right there while he turns out a sample so that we can approve the shape and texture. We work with color samples. Then we go back a few days later to check that the finish, shape and metal findings are exactly as we want them.

Our rug buyers and fashion coordinators go to the farthest corners of the earth: To bazaars in Damascus, to Morocco, to Persia, to India. They go to small villages and work with fine hand-craftsmen in order to find or have made exciting and unusual pieces. Sometimes they go with an idea or samples or sketches. Or samples are sent ahead. When they arrive at some remote village in India they go to look at the samples that have been made for Bloomingdale's.

Sometimes we have collections done by great contemporary designers, or we work with them, suggesting new categories of merchandise that could be important in today's living. Merchandise managers, buyers, fashion coordinators work not only on design ideas they have developed themselves but with designers all over the world. Too, we rely on technical knowledge from experts outside the store to add to the internal merchandising expertise. The time, travel, imagination and attention to detail add up to a staggering amount of work.

Because a large store like Bloomingdale's has tremendous buying power all over the world, not only are you offered unusual variety but the chances are the merchandise is available to you at better prices than you're apt to find elsewhere.

Anyone coming into Bloomingdale's could find furnishings for his entire house: Glassware from all over the world, great collections of tablecloths and napkins, china, pottery—old and new—even superb Oriental treasures. Someone, some specific someone with great taste, has hand selected each individual item. And that's not the easiest thing in the world to do. You buy two rice bowls from one dealer. You go to another for a dozen plates, six saucers and one platter. To buy one entire collection of Imari porcelain, for example, a buyer must spend days and days searching through several cities.

I have heard people say, "Oh, I'm not going to buy that now. I'll wait till I go to Japan and buy it there." But a Bloomingdale's expert will spend endless days going through the markets of Japan, from the big cities to remote little towns. How could a tourist hope to duplicate this procedure? Most resources are not right out on the streets. They're in back alleys, in towns that are hard to find. Our buyers know where to go and whom to go to. I have gone in search of treasures for myself and even with good connections and considerable knowledge I haven't been able to find them.

When it comes to deciding what to buy for your home and where to put it, after you have done your own hard thinking and planning, it is perhaps wisest to rely on the professionals in a department store where there is a staff of consultants and interior designers who can answer your questions or become completely involved with you in designing an entire room, an entire house, a number of houses.

So the time has come to decorate! You could do no better than to take your problems and ideas to a fine department store. Everything you need is probably there under one roof: The variety, the taste, the range of mood, the technical knowledge.

a short dictionary of decorating terms

Aalto, Alvar
Finnish architect and designer. In the 1930s originated a technique for making furniture by laminating thin layers of birch wood under pressure. He also designed molded plywood body-contoured chairs that could be mass-produced.

Acanthus
This leaf was a motif used by the Greeks, particularly on the capitals of Corinthian columns.

Accent lighting
A technique used to call attention to specific features in a room by means of a beam of light concentrated on one object or one area of a room.

Accent rug
Sometimes called an area rug, and used in one area of a room to call attention to a furniture grouping or to provide a color accent.

Acrylic
Any of a number of manmade fibers with trademarked names such as Acrilan, Creslan or Orlon. Acrylic is widely used in wearing apparel for men and women as well as for upholstery, curtains and carpeting. Its virtues are its stain and soil resistance, its resiliency and its ability to hold shape without sagging or stretching. Further, it is quick-drying and long-wearing. Solid sheet acrylics with trademarked names such as Lucite and Plexiglas are used for many purposes, from furniture to room dividers.

African art
An increasingly popular collector's field, African art is predominantly sculpture and carving in clay, metal, stone, ivory or wood, most of it highly stylized.

Akari lanterns
Isamu Noguchi, the Japanese-American sculptor, has created splendid works of art in lampshades constructed in the traditional paper-and-rib techniques. Akari is the registered name for these lanterns—**akari** being the Japanese word for light.

Alabaster
A slightly translucent stone with a milky color used for architectural adornment as well as statuary.

Alpujarra (ahl-poo-Harr-ah)
An area in southern Spain where rugs and bedspreads have been hand loomed by the peasants since the 15th century. The rugs are so coarse and heavy that though they were originally intended as bedspreads, they are used on floors today. The designs are very bold and rendered in intense colors.

Antimacassar
Literally "against Macassar," which was an oil that men used for hair grooming in the Victorian era. Thus were born the small panels of embroidered material, or crochet and lace, that went on the backs of chairs to protect them from hair oil. Fussy as the Victorians were, matching protective covers for the arms of chairs naturally followed.

Antique
For import purposes any home furnishings or works of art are defined as antique if they are one hundred or more years old, according to the U.S. Customs regulations. This definition is held generally even if antiques are domestic in origin.

Apothecary jars
Although originally these jars held medicinal ingredients for apothecaries, today they're apt to hold flour and sugar on a kitchen shelf. Fine ones abound. Lambeth jars in blue delft earthenware are among the rarest, as are early medieval ones of green glazed pottery. There are some very beautiful apothecary jars being made today in Spain and Portugal.

Applied decoration
Anything attached to the face of furniture for ornamentation, such as wood, moldings, metal designs or motifs. These are usually applied with glue or tiny nails.

Appliqué

A familiar needlework term for a cut-out design of fabric applied to a contrasting material.

Apron

Usually a decorative board or band of wood that is placed under a tabletop, the seat of a chair, the underside of a shelf or the base of a cabinet.

Armoire (ahrm-Wahr)

The originals were the dominant piece of furniture in French country homes, designed to hold clothes, linens, silver, dinnerware, even food. Some contend these were an old version of the modern "hope chest." The traditional version is built on a strong architectural frame and stands on low legs, with long double doors from top to base. Another version, called the *armoire de deux corps*, is built in two sections, the upper one taller than the lower, with double doors on both. In today's decoration, armoires serve to hold a lot of things besides clothing (although I still love them used for that purpose in a bedroom). I particularly like some version of the armoire used in a room plan for the bulk it lends in furniture balance and arrangement.

Art glass

Generally any piece of glass that is meant to be looked at rather than used. The shapes can be quite unusual, the colors quite imaginative. Most art glass dates to the late 1800s, and includes sandwich, hobnail, satin, peachblow and others from America and abroad.

Artifact

Ancient objects manmade of stone, bone, clay, ceramic or metal.

Ash

A blond hardwood that I particularly like to use on walls in its natural, rough-sawn state because of the texture and color it brings to a room. Ash is also used in the frames of chairs—from Windsor to the most contemporary designs.

Astragal molding

Today the term is used to describe the convex wood molding on the edge of a cabinet door, although the original architectural term indicated a small semicircular or torus molding.

Atrium

The courtyard or entrance hall of a classical Roman house, usually with the roof or part of it open to the sky.

Aubergine (oh-bare-Zheen)

French for the deep color of ripe eggplant. Specifically it refers to the glaze of Ming dynasty porcelains. Not only is it a splendid color in high-glaze ceramics, it can also be used as a background or an accent color in a room.

Aubusson (oh-bew-Sohn) rugs

Named after the tapestry works at Aubusson, France, in the Middle Ages. Some of the early patterns were Oriental in origin. The Aubusson carpet woven in wool, linen and cotton was a particular favorite in the Louis XIV period. The patterns were large in scale, rendered in soft, muted colors. Today an Aubusson carpet can be anything that has a coarse tapestry weave in either traditional or contemporary patterns.

Austrian shade

Curtain of sheer, vertically shirred fabric which is pulled up the window like a regular shade, but hung on vertical cords rather than the customary roller. Austrian shades had a flurry of popularity a few years back, but their look is a little too opulent for today's decorating, and Roman shades seem more suitable.

Axminster

Carpet originally made in Axminster, England, or any carpet with thick high pile and a stiff jute back. The weave makes possible colorful and intricate patterns. Axminster usually ranges from 27-inch strip carpeting to 18-foot broadloom.

Azulejos (ah-soo-Lay-hoess)

From the Spanish word—*azul*—for blue. These are intricately patterned tiles, originally done in the favorite 17th-century colors of blue and white. Today these tiles are made in Spain, Mexico and Portugal and are traditionally used in bathrooms, kitchens, dining rooms and garden rooms. Azulejos come in all manner of colors and designs, from abstract patterns to graphic scenes and heraldry.

Baccarat (bah-kah-Rah)

The crystal of the French kings. Baccarat is made with highly sophisticated techniques of cutting, pressing and blowing, and is much prized by collectors. It has been made in France since the early 1700s.

Bachelor chest
Introduced during the Queen Anne period (early 18th century), the bachelor chest is designed to hold a man's haberdashery, and usually has a top that pulls out or folds over to serve as a desk area or to hold toiletries.

Bahut (bah-Hoo)
A traditional French country piece used as a small buffet with two drawers across the top and two doors below. Usually about 42 inches high and 48 inches long. Popular in the 17th and 18th centuries.

Bail handle
A drawer or door pull shaped like the bail or loop on a door knocker or escutcheon. This design for drawer hardware originated in the 17th century.

Baker's rack
Originally used by bakers to display their wares, they're used today in every kind of room to hold almost anything except bread. The better ones are characterized by brass shelves and wrought-iron back and sides.

Baldachino (bahl-dah-Keen-o)
The raised canopy above an altar. Its present-day application is as a half-canopy over a bed. (See the Saturday Generation room on page 147.)

Baluster
An upright support for a banister, usually turned or carved in an urn shape.

Bamboo furniture
English furniture of the 18th century that was made to look like bamboo but was actually carved or turned of beech wood. Sometimes it was painted to look like natural bamboo, sometimes in vibrant colors. Although transitional in period, bamboo furniture can be used today in almost any room from traditional to ultra modern. (See photos on pages 122 and 123.)

Bamboo-turned
As above, the technique of turning wood on a lathe to imitate bamboo.

Banding
A narrow inlay of wood that runs around the edge of a tabletop, on desks or around drawers.

Banister-back chair
A late 17th-century American chair, the back of which had uprights that resembled banister supports at a stairway. Sometimes these upright spindles were full round, sometimes split.

Banquette (bahng-Kett)
Early forms were simply an upholstered bench with or without a back. Today's designs are very versatile and come in a variety of moods, sizes and shapes. They are an excellent device for modular seating and can be seen in many of the rooms in this book, specifically pages 106, 107, 108.

Barcelona chair
A classic of contemporary design created by Ludwig Mies van der Rohe for the Barcelona Exposition in 1929, and characterized by a stainless steel frame and upholstered leather back and seat.

Barn siding
Weathered and gray driftwoody planks from old barns, particularly in New England. Often used for interior walls for a country atmosphere.

Baroque
A style of florid architecture, art, music and decoration which originated in Italy during the late 16th century and spread rapidly across all Europe, characterized by large-scale, bold detail, sweeping curves, heavy ornamentation and twisted columns.

Basalt
An inky-black Wedgwood porcelain, still being made at the Wedgwood factory in England, that resembles a dark-brown igneous rock. The styles and shapes are classic 18th-century Wedgwood, usually self-patterned in relief.

Baseboard
Horizontal wood trim around the bottom of a wall. It can be as low as two inches, as high as twelve inches.

Bas-relief
Semi-round sculpture which is not free-standing but is attached to a wall.

239

Batik

A hand-printed fabric usually of cotton that is characteristic of the Dutch East Indies and Malaysia, produced by hand dipping the fabric into dyes after elements of the design have been coated with wax to be dye-resistant.

Batiste

A sheer, fine, plain cotton fabric that can be used for curtains and bed hangings. Usually in solid colors, but sometimes printed with designs or woven in stripes.

Batten

Bracing strips of wood nailed across vertical boards, as in board-and-batten doors, for a room with a country look.

Bauhaus (Bow-house)

A school of architecture and design established in Weimar, Germany, in 1919 that has had a lasting influence on 20th-century art, architecture, furniture and industrial design.

Beading

A molding or ornament that looks like a string of beads. It is used to decorate flat or plain surfaces.

Beam

A long piece of timber or metal used to support a roof or ceiling. But beams can be purely ornamental and be applied to boxlike rooms, as you can see in photo after photo in this book.

Bennington

Pottery that originated in Bennington, Vermont, in the 19th century. It is widely collected and used today. The most familiar pattern is the mottled brown ware with an almost marbleized effect.

Bergère (bear-Zhair)

One of the few traditional 18th-century pieces that remain popular today, the bergère is an upholstered arm chair with closed, upholstered sides. Although it is essentially traditional, the use of contemporary fabrics and intense colors on the wooden frame can give it an up-to-date look.

Bessarabian rug

Tapestry-woven or knotted-pile rug made in Rumania during the 18th and 19th centuries. The designs are characterized by vivid colored floral patterns against dark backgrounds.

Bevel

The rounded edge of any flat surface—e.g., the metal rim of a tabletop or the edge of a mirror. When the bevel is used near the foot of a chair or table leg it is called a chamfer.

Bibelot (bib-Low)

Literally a plaything. A small ornamental object.

Bible box

This desklike piece of furniture started out to be what its name implies—a box to hold the family Bible. It was made with a slanting top to serve as a reading stand. Legs were added later to form a lectern or desk.

Bibliothèque (bib-lee-oh-Take)

French for a capacious bookcase. This large piece of furniture is suitable for balancing heavy architectural elements in a room, because it is architectural in itself.

Bisque

White porcelain left unglazed in its sandy natural finish. Bisque may be used for crockery, urns, even sculptural figures.

Blackamoor

A sculptural turbaned Negro figure, elaborately costumed and painted, sometimes holding a candelabra, sometimes supporting a tabletop, sometimes used as a hitching post. Highly favored in the early 18th century and the Victorian era.

Blanc de chine (blang duh sheen)

Chinese porcelain with a very high glaze, usually in soft tones of white, used for Foo dogs, lotus bowls and figures of the goddess Kuan Yin.

Bleached finishes

Wood that may be dark in its natural state can be lightened with special chemicals. The wood texture becomes more evident when bleached. After bleaching a sealer can be applied and the bleached finish is permanent.

Block printing

The slow hand process of applying a pattern or picture to fabric with a series of carved wood blocks coated with dye. Most fabrics are machine printed today.

Bobêche (bow-Behsh)
A small saucerlike rim at the top of a candlestick intended to catch the candle drippings. Some are glass and ornamented with crystal pendants. Others are of the same material as the candlestick.

Body
The basic material of a piece of pottery or porcelain before the glaze or finish is applied.

Boiserie (bwah-zeh-Ree)
The French term for fine 18th-century paneling and decorative woodwork. Over the years the term has come to mean any wood paneling.

Bolection molding
One or a series of heavy moldings applied to the front of a fireplace or chimney breast.

Bombé (bohm-Bay)
Most commonly used to describe the bulge on the front or sides—or both—of a Regence or Louis XV commode.

Bonheur du jour (boh-Nuhr duh zhoor)
A small French lady's writing desk, typical of the Louis XVI period. It has a small cabinet top with a drop front for writing, and slender, tapered Louis XVI legs.

Bonnet top
The arched contour at the top of armoires, secretaries, clocks and such.

Bonnetière (bohn-neh-tee-Yair)
An 18th-century piece specifically built to hold a collection of lady's hats. It is narrow and tall, and versions are used today for books or collections of objects, much as an armoire is.

Boss
The projecting ornament placed at the intersection of beams or moldings. It's often a carved head or an animal or cherub, flower or foliage motif.

Bouillotte (boo-Yacht) lamp
A candle lamp of gilt or painted metal with a shallow painted tole shade, originally hung or set over a bouillotte table. A very popular lamp today. I am particularly fond of the shape of the very shallow bouillotte lampshade with its slightly slanted sides.

Bouillotte table
A Louis XVI circular game table, generally made of mahogany with openwork brass gallery and trim and a marble top. An extra top, or bouchon, covered on one side with leather and on the other with baize cloth, provided a playing surface.

Boulle (bool)
Inlay of brass in wood or tortoise shell. It was named after Louis XVI's cabinetmaker, André Charles Boulle. Also spelled buhl.

Bracket
A flat-topped prop, usually iron, which projects from a wall to support a beam or other architectural member above it.

Brasses
General term referring to hardware such as drawer pulls and escutcheons.

Breakfront
A big bookcase or cabinet with the bottom section enclosed by doors, the top either open or glass-paned. Usually the center section projects (or breaks) forward beyond the two end sections.

Breuer, Marcel
Architect and designer and one of the leaders of the Bauhaus movement. His chrome-plated steel and leather armchair, designed in 1925 and a contemporary classic, has been a major influence on the design of modern furniture.

Broadloom
Solid-color or patterned carpeting woven on a broad loom in widths of nine, twelve, fifteen and eighteen feet. The quality is determined by the closeness of the tufts and the number of rows per inch.

Bronze doré
French term for gilt bronze or bronze that has been gold-plated.

Buffet (bew-Fay)
A piece of dining room furniture set against the wall to hold food and serving dishes. Originally a 15th-century Italian cupboard, it developed during the 17th and 18th centuries into several different pieces of furniture. Today the term is a general one and can refer to a sideboard or a dresser, a side table or even a more up-to-date piece for storing linens, china, and silver.

Bun foot

A type of foot you'll see on early-17th-century furniture, it looks like a slightly flattened ball—or bun.

Burl

An abnormal or diseased growth on trees. When thinly sawed and used as a veneer, it gives an effect of mottled or swirled configurations rather than ordinary graining.

Burlap

A coarse fabric woven of hemp or jute fibers that comes in a tremendous range of width and colors. It enjoyed considerable popularity as a drapery and wall fabric in the 1950s and '60s, but many who used burlap discovered that it shrinks when cleaned. Today there are paper-backed burlaps available.

Burnt sienna, burnt umber

Burnt sienna, a yellow-brown, and burnt umber, a dark blue-brown, are pigments used in mixing paints for interiors to deepen and "gray" the color.

Butler's tray

A large wooden serving tray "fenced in" either by a wooden gallery or by hinged flaps which can be lowered to extend the surface. Originally used—as the name implies—by butlers, today it can serve as a coffee table resting on a folding wood base.

Cabriole (kah-bree-Ole)

A furniture leg shaped like the leg of an animal— swelling outward at the knee, inward at the ankle and ending in a short flare like an animal's foot. First seen in 17th-century Europe during the Baroque period, it turned up again in the work of 18th-century furniture designers and is the distinguishing detail of Louis XV and Queen Anne furniture.

Cachepot (kahsh-Poh)

A container of porcelain, tole or other metals which hides the ordinary flowerpot inside it.

Camel back

Chair back of the late Chippendale or Hepplewhite style. The top rail is humped in a serpentine curve.

Campaign chest

A portable chest of drawers with brassbound corners and handles at either side used in the late 18th century to store the gear of field officers in the British army. The chests were made as both single and stacking units and the upper unit was often fitted as a writing desk. Because they were so functional and unornamented they have been widely copied in various materials for use in contemporary interiors.

Canapé (kan-nah-Pay)

A piece of furniture that was probably covered with a canopy (hence the name) and used as a daybed, but today is a sofa or couch with a back whose curve continues into the curving arms.

Cane

A flexible material made from rattan that has been split and woven for use in chair backs and seats. It first appeared in England, in the late 17th century (imported by the East India Company) and has since turned up on everything from Louis XV open arm chairs to Victorian bentwood dining furniture. Today the pattern of woven cane has been printed on fabric and wallpaper and woven into carpeting.

Canopy

The wooden frame and fabric hangings over a bed such as a four-poster. Canopies are also used for indoor and outdoor awning effects and in rooms that are tented.

Cantilever

A beam supported near the center and weighted at one end, while the other end projects without apparent support. The cantilever principle can be used in many architectural ways.

Canton

Oriental export china brought to this country in the late 18th century, when the China trade flourished. Usually blue and white, Canton is still popular and the traditional designs have been copied in wallpaper and fabrics.

Canvas

Usually found in outdoor awnings and canopies, canvas is used today for slipcovers, upholstery, and wall and window treatments. This rough and tough fabric is usually cotton, though it can be woven of linen. The natural fibers take color brilliantly.

Capital

The architectural element at the top of a column. In today's decorating the addition of columns with capitals appropriate to the rest of the room can lend a great deal of architectural interest.

Cartouche (kahr-Toosh)

A shield or egg-shaped form used as an ornament or design element, sometimes surrounded with elaborate wreathes, garlands or scrolls.

Carved rug

A rug whose pile is cut at varying heights to achieve a carved effect, sometimes in a border design, sometimes as an allover pattern.

Caryatid (Kahr-yah-teed)

A supporting column that is sculptured in the form of a woman's figure. Originally a Greek architectural device, caryatids could later be found on table legs, mantels, paneling, bedposts and even as bases for lamps.

Case goods

This is a professional furniture term for storage pieces —as opposed to upholstered seating pieces. Case goods can be dining room, bedroom or living room furniture, and are usually made of wood.

Casement cloth

A lightweight, sheer fabric used for glass curtains.

Casement window

A window hinged at either the top or the side so that it swings out and in. The glass panes are usually small and leaded.

Cassone (kah-So-ney)

A large Italian chest decorated with carvings, inlays or paint.

Celadon

Chinese porcelain with a glaze in colors that vary from jade to clear gray.

Chair rail

A strip of molding placed on a wall at the exact height of the top of a chair back to protect the wall from scrapes. It also serves as a divider between the dado (lower paneling) and the upper wall.

Chair table

A table with a hinged back section which is usually raised but can be dropped into a horizontal position to extend the table surface. Also called a monk's chair, it dates from the 17th century.

Chaise longue (shez Lohng)

This can be an elongated chair, a deep bergère chair with matching upholstered ottoman, or an ottoman bridging two arm chairs.

Chaise percée (shez peer-Say)

A chair with cane seat, sides and back which—in the Louis XV era—served to hide a chamber pot under its lift-up seat.

Charger

In medieval times the servant who served the bigger joints of meat was called the charger. Gradually the term has come to mean any big, flat serving dish or plate big enough to hold a major menu item. Chargers are usually of pewter or silver, although they can be made of decorated pottery as well.

Charles X

The type of pale, honey-colored fruitwood furniture in simple Empire style that was first made during the reign of this French king (1824–30).

Chenille carpet

Most custom wall-to-wall carpeting is chenille. It has probably the most luxurious texture—and is the longest-wearing—of any pile carpeting. In widths up to thirty feet, it can be woven in any design or color.

Chesterfield

A large, overstuffed, completely upholstered sofa.

Cheval glass

A portable full-length mirror swinging from two vertical posts that are part of a trestle. Some smaller versions have a drawer between the posts and are meant to sit atop a chest or table.

Chevron

Molding typical of Norman and Romanesque architecture, so called because of the repetition of a series of "V" shapes. Sometimes known as zigzag.

Chiavari chair (k'yah-Vah-ree)

Originating in Chiavari, Italy, this is a simple, lightweight, mass-produced chair with a rush seat, which follows a basic design by Gio Ponti.

Chinese Chippendale

An 18th-century English furniture style of the Chippendale school which featured Chinese materials and designs, using such details as dragon feet on chairs and tables, beds and cabinets with pagoda tops, Oriental lacquer finishes, and chair backs with fretwork designs.

Chinese red
The glistening, vibrant orange-red found in Oriental lacquer, today usually used as an accent color.

Chinoiserie (sheen-wah-zay-Ree)
The 18th-century French term for things Chinese or things that look Chinese. Today it refers generally to furniture with lacquered or painted designs in Chinese motifs.

Chintz
This thin cotton fabric—glazed, more often than not, and generally printed in bright floral patterns—has been around since the 18th century.

Chippendale (1740–99)
Thomas Chippendale II, son and father of a family of cabinetmakers, created what was certainly the outstanding style of the Georgian period. Chippendale started with the English, French and Chinese sources current in his time, but developed his own variations. He preferred to work in mahogany, but many of his pieces were lacquered or gilded, even veneered occasionally.

Claw-and-ball foot
The original inspiration came from China and represented a dragon's talons gripping a round jewel. It was first used in Europe in many of the early Chippendale pieces in which the cabriole leg ends in a bird's claw holding a ball.

Commode
French term for a chest of drawers. The Victorians, with their love of delicate euphemism, used the word for a stool or box that concealed a chamber pot.

Console table
The unsung hero in furniture. I am inordinately fond of the console table, as you will see all through this book, particularly in the section on furniture arranging. A console table is generally much longer than wide, can be rounded or rectangular, comes in every style, and is nearly indispensable in a furniture grouping in the center of the room, or in a wall grouping beneath a painting or mirror. Ordinarily one of the long sides of a console table is backed against a wall or a sofa.

Conversation group
A calculated arrangement of furniture, which can

include banquettes, sofas, chairs, large and small tables, grouped together for convenient conversation.

Conversation pit
A padded recess sunk into the floor or surrounded by higher platforms, ordinarily three- or four-sided, to serve the same purpose as the conversation group, above.

Cornice
A decorative element shaped like a crown that is usually used instead of a valance as an ornamental border above windows. Also used for the decorative trim crowning a piece of furniture.

Coromandel screen
Coromandel is a stretch of the southeast India coast, but the screen itself is Chinese in origin. The famous East India Company used to ship the screens to Europe from Coromandel ports. They are made of several panels, heavily lacquered in deep, dark tones and decorated with bas-relief figures, houses, flowers or landscapes.

Cove
Another word for cornice (see above), usually used to refer to the concave element that joins the ceiling to the top of the wall.

Cupboard bed
A bed surrounded on three sides by a wooden enclosure intended to protect the sleeper from drafts. Originally, in provincial France and Italy, the cupboard was a storage piece much like the armoire.

Cupola
A dome at the apex of a roof that can be a skylight or be used structurally to break up a long horizontal line. I call your attention to the *treillage* room on page 22.

Custom
Decorator's word for anything that is specifically designed and made to order. Example: Custom draperies, as opposed to ready-to-hang.

Cutting
Used to indicate a small sample of fabric. Sometimes called a swatch.

Dado
The lower portion of a wall that is decorated with

wood paneling, wallpaper or paint and separated from the wall above it by a chair rail.

Damask
A fabric, made on a special loom known as a Jacquard, that is self-patterned and usually of only one color. Damask can be woven of cotton, wool, silk, synthetic fibers or linen. I think it's particularly handsome and more up to date when woven of natural linen and either plain or printed.

Davenport
An earthenware stone china made in Longport, England, from 1793 to 1822.

Denim
A durable heavy cotton twill fabric that is available in nearly every hue of the rainbow, and in many textures—some brushed to look nearly like suede.

Dentils
A row of evenly spaced cubes that look like projecting teeth standing out from cornice molding.

Derby
English porcelains made from 1756 to 1848 at Derby, Bow and Chelsea. Pieces treasured by collectors include plain white or painted and gilded figurines, and elaborate table services, some of which look very much like Japanese Imari. The three most notable types are Crown Derby, Bloor Derby and Royal Crown Derby.

Directoire (dee-rek-t'Wahr) (1795–1804)
This transitional furniture style was born between the fall of Robespierre and the rise of Napoleon. It was predominantly straight-lined, and the classical curves were very restrained. Two outstanding examples are the Recamier chaise longue and the folding campaign chair. Local walnut and fruitwood were used instead of imported mahogany, as were combinations of metals.

Director's chair
A folding portable chair with X-shaped turned legs, the back and seat made of canvas, leather or plastic.

Distressed
A finish on furniture or beams contrived to make them look old and worn. The finish can be achieved with awls or adzes, by beating with chains and sometimes by quite extreme treatments such as peppering the wood with buckshot.

Do-it-yourself furniture
Not, as you might think, made in home workshops but separate units that can be assembled like Tinker Toys or Erector sets to create various pieces of furniture and different furniture arrangements. You'll see several examples in Chapter 15, The Saturday Generation.

Doulton
Originally a very simple 19th-century stoneware with a salt glaze, Doulton soon became more decorative and arty. In 1901 it was decreed Royal Doulton by Edward VII. Since then Royal Doulton has launched many fine finishes including *rouge flambé*, *sang de boeuf* and crackle glazes produced by the glazing and coloring techniques of the Sung and Ming potters of China. The most familiar Royal Doulton pieces are the popular figurines and Toby mugs.

Dovetail
A method of joining wood used widely in drawer construction. The sides, back and front of the drawer are notched in a feather pattern (of a dove's tail) and interlock tightly at 45-degree angles.

Dowel
A peg used to join wooden furniture elements.

Duck
A heavy plain fabric much like canvas, which comes in many colors, both solid and print, and is suitable for furniture upholstery and slipcovers (both indoors and out).

Dust ruffle
A shirred, pleated or tailored ruffle attached to a bedspread, box spring or the rails of a bed to hide the legs or frame and give a more boxy look from top to bottom. It's sometimes called a petticoat or flounce.

Eames, Charles
American industrial designer and architect, famous for the now classic prize-winning chair (designed with Eero Saarinen) which is constructed of molded plywood forms on a metal frame. Other familiar Eames chairs are the fiberglass shell, the wire cage and a traditional club chair and ottoman in black hide. Eames is one of the strongest influences on furniture design in this century.

Earthenware
Pottery made from baked earth or clay, of which the best-known types are 17th-century delftware with a tin glaze and the cream-colored queen's ware produced by Josiah Wedgwood.

Easy-care
A class of fabrics that are either blends of natural and synthetic fibers or have been chemically treated so that they regain their original appearance after washing with little or no ironing. Many easy-care fabrics are used in curtains and bedspreads.

Ébeniste (eh-beh-Nist)
French word for cabinetmaker, deriving from ebony—or *ébène*—the favored wood for furniture during the French Renaissance. Guilds of *ébenistes* were organized as protection from foreign craftsmen who cut prices. The guilds set up a committee for quality control, and from 1741 craftsmen were allowed to stamp their work with their name or initials.

Ebony
A dark, brownish-black wood that comes from various tropical countries—Africa, India and Ceylon. In Europe it became a favored wood for veneers, particularly with the French *ébenistes* and the English 18th-century cabinetmakers. Fine pianos are traditionally made of ebony.

Eclecticism
In decorating, a mix—choosing suitably from several styles and periods.

Edwardian
The furniture and decorating style of the extravagant and sybaritic period of King Edward VII of England (1901–10).

Egg and dart
One of the most widely used carved ornamentations for woodwork and furniture. Deriving from Greek architectural detail of the 5th century B.C., it is a row of dart-and-egg shapes.

Elevation
A two-dimensional scale drawing of a wall, side or upright section of a building.

Elizabethan
Fundamentally Gothic, with touches of Italian Renaissance, Elizabethan furniture can be identified by bulbous, melon-shaped table legs, channeled decoration and the use of the Tudor rose in ornamentation.

Elm
A hardwood like oak, in a similar light-brown shade, that takes stain and polish beautifully, and is used frequently as a veneer. Many 18th-century English pieces were constructed of elm—sometimes in combination with yew wood.

Embossing
Sometimes called repoussé, embossing is a technique of surface decoration, in which a design is stamped, hammered or molded from the reverse side of a sheet of metal. Embossing was used in the late 19th century on tin ceilings, metal cornices and even silver hollowware.

Enamel
The word has become associated mostly with paint, when actually it originated as a ceramic glaze that was colored and elaborately designed. This finish was applied to metal, and there are many beautiful examples: Enamel tableware from China and the exquisite antique Battersea enamel boxes.

Entablature
An architectural term for the part of a classical order above the columns, consisting of an architrave, frieze and cornice. More likely than not the entablature is elaborately decorated, carved and molded.

Escutcheon
Originally a shield on which a coat of arms was displayed, "escutcheon" has now come to mean the metal plate over a keyhole or behind a handle.

Étagère (eh-tah-Jere)
A cabinet whose open shelves are used to display books, collections, objets d'art. A very popular piece of furniture today in wood, metal, glass and combinations The original étagère was pyramid-shaped and called a whatnot by the Victorians.

Façade
The front elevation of a building, sometimes much more elaborate than the building deserves—hence the term "putting up a good front."

Faïence (fah-Yahnse)
Faenza was the Italian center for majolica in the Renaissance. The French variation of the word has

come to mean a tin-glazed or tin-enameled earthenware popular throughout Europe from the 16th to the 18th centuries. Delft is one type, majolica another.

Faille
A fabric of either silk, wool or synthetic fibers woven for a flat, ribbed look.

Fauteuil (foh-Toy)
A French open armchair with wooden arms, its seat and back either upholstered or caned, in contrast to the bergère, which is completely upholstered.

Faux bois (foh bwah)
Literally fake wood: A technique of painting a door or wall to resemble wood.

Faux marbre (foh Mahr-bruh)
Fake marble, again achieved by paint. Also called marbleizing.

Felt
A fabric manufactured by matting wool, mohair or a mixture of fibers under heat and pressure. Felt comes as yardage in many widths and in almost any color you can think of. It is used for upholstery, table covers, bedspreads, even curtains, but it is difficult to clean.

Fender
Originally a strictly functional metal fence around a fireplace to prevent logs and coals from escaping. Gradually the fender got more and more elaborate, with the addition of scrolls, piercing and adornments to match those of the andirons and fire screen. Mostly brass, although some fenders are crafted of steel and even—grandly—silver.

Festoon
A loop of fabric draped above a window, or a similar carved shape to adorn a piece of furniture.

Filigree
A delicate openwork pattern that is either cut in wood or punched out in metal.

Fillet
An architectural term for a narrow, flat strip of wood or stone that separates two carved moldings of a column. It can also be a band that ends a series of moldings. In cabinetwork the word refers to a rectangular section of wood molding.

Finial
Most often in the shape of a pineapple or a knob, the finial is found on top of a post, bedpost, or bracket of a lamp.

Finish
Paint, lacquer, varnish applied to a wood surface, both to decorate and to protect the wood, are the classic finishes; today technology has introduced many different substances, and new ones are appearing all the time.

Fir
A soft wood, usually from the northwestern section of the U.S., which is used to manufacture plywood and is sometimes used for the framework of inexpensive furniture.

Fitzhugh
The Earl of Fitzhugh lent his name to a kind of Oriental porcelain originally made for him. It has a border of pomegranates and bees. Today the pattern has been re-created by Spode and other companies.

Flame stitch
Also called point d'Hongrie. A needlepoint pattern which originated in Hungary, resembling the outline of flames.

Flat arch
An arch that has only a very slight curve.

Flock design
A design achieved by felting the surface of fabric or wallpaper to create the appearance of cut velvet.

Fluting
Parallel grooves or channels in a column or furniture leg. When these channels are raised from the surface, they are known as reeding.

Flyspecking
Because antiques actually have flyspecks on them as a result of untidy housekeeping, many distressed finishes seek to imitate this authentic detail.

Foil papers
Wallpapers or other paper coverings with a metal surface, such as Japanese tea chest paper. Today there are many bold contemporary designs in wallpaper that have a metallic glint.

Footman

Not a servant at all, no more than a silent butler is. The footman is a stand of brass or steel in either oblong or oval shape that stood in front of the fireplace to keep dishes hot before serving, much as a hot tray does today.

Formica

The trade name for a rigid laminated plastic-over-wood that is used for tabletops, counters, shelves, even as paneling around a sink work area, and is available in many patterns and colors.

French bed

Also called the sleigh bed. A 19th-century design with a high footboard and headboard, sometimes canopied.

French door, window or casement

Two multi-paned vertical windows that are hung from the sides, go down to the floor and open like the halves of a double door. They can be used as ordinary windows, but usually open onto a balcony, terrace, patio or garden.

French Empire (ahm-Peer) (1804–15)

A furniture and furnishings style originating with Napoleon and leaning heavily on the design inspiration of Greek and Roman pieces, with a little touch here and there of Egyptian. There were bronze and gilt ornamentations. Table legs often sported human figures, griffins and lions. Marble was used, as was dark mahogany. The Napoleonic emblem of the letter *N* surrounded by the victor's wreath was frequently used, and is almost a symbol of the Empire style. Traces of this style found their way into other periods and styles, such as English Victorian, German Biedermeier and American Federal.

French heading

A topping for curtains or draperies, pleated or gathered at intervals of five or six inches and stitched together about four inches from the top.

French polish

A very high-gloss shellac finish.

French Provincial

No such thing—that is, no *one* such thing. Provincial styles in furniture were more primitive copies of the court pieces.

French Regence (reh-Zhahnss) (1715–23)

A transitional style that began during the regency of Philippe, Duc d'Orléans, and bridged the grandeur of Louis XIV and the more graceful Louis XV. This period marked the entry of the cabriole leg with a doe foot and of storage pieces such as the secretaire, chiffonier and commode.

Fresco

A technique of mural painting in which water-soluble colors are applied to wet plaster while it is still fresh (*fresco*).

Fretwork

A cut-out pattern in wood or metal used in doorways, window treatments, even room dividers. Fretwork can be very ethnic in feeling—Moorish—and suit any period.

Frieze

A horizontal band decorated with carving or sculpture and set between the architrave and cornice of a building. The word can also refer to a wide decorative strip at the top of a wall.

Fruitwood

Wood from a fruit tree—apple, cherry, pear and others—most often found in small pieces of furniture in the country style, fruit trees being smaller than larger trees used for lumber. Today fruitwood is used mostly in veneers.

Furring

Thin strips of wood applied to a wall to support paneling, wallboard or shelves.

Gallery

The railing around the edge of a table, a serving tray or a shelf, usually ornamental. "Gallery" can also refer to a long hallway hung with pictures.

Galloon

A narrow ribbon or braid used to trim curtains or upholstery.

Gate-leg table

A table with one or two hinged leaves and one or two legs that swing out like a gate to support the leaves when they are raised. When the legs are closed and the leaves dropped, the table takes up very little space.

Geometric print

A pattern for fabric or wallpaper composed of diamonds, circles, triangles, rectangles, more contemporary in mood than, say, a floral print.

Gesso (Jes-o)

Finely ground plaster, mixed with water and formed into decorations for moldings, walls or furniture. When it dries, it's painted or gilded.

Gilding

The technique of making plaster, stone, wood or metal look like gold. The Egyptians applied a thin layer of beaten gold to such surfaces and thus originated gold leaf. Later we find water gilding, oil gilding and—in the case of metal—fire gilding, though modern technology has developed the technique of plating metal. Now most furniture is gilded by applying gold leaf with a fixative and burnishing.

Gimp

Flat decorative tape used to trim and hide upholstery tacks or the stitching in draperies.

Gingham

A yarn-dyed fabric in crisp stripes or checks.

Glass curtains

Sheer curtains of any translucent material, from silk gauze to fiberglass kept drawn across windows to filter light and give privacy.

Glaze

A fine, transparent glass coating that is fired on pottery, porcelain and stoneware to give a hard, shiny, non-porous finish. The Chinese were the masters of the art, unchallenged for their richness and range of colors. A similar glaze can be applied to furniture and walls to give a finish like china.

Glazed chintz

A plain or printed cotton fabric, one surface of which is coated with a paraffin or by a calendering technique that stiffens the fabric and gives it a high sheen.

Glazing

A hard finish produced by either varnish or shellac to tone down the base color of a paint.

Gothic (1100–1500)

Like its counterpart the towering Gothic cathedral, Gothic furniture displayed pointed arches, buttress shapes, pillars with molding details. It was made of heavy carved oak, usually left unpolished.

Graining

A technique of painting a surface to simulate the natural grain and color of wood which can serve to disguise inferior wood or plain plaster. Also called *faux bois*.

Graphics or graphic arts

Engravings, etchings, woodcuts, silk screen prints or lithographs. The value of graphics depends on how many copies of each design have been printed. The fewer copies, the higher the price.

Grass cloth

A cloth woven of grass and then glued to a paper backing to make a particularly beautiful wall covering. Invented by the Chinese some two thousand years ago, it can be found today in a great variety of colors and weaves, even with metallic paper grounds.

Grosgrain

Silk, cotton or synthetic-fiber fabric with a ribbed surface, used mostly for trimming but also used for bedspreads, curtains and even upholstery.

Gros point (gro point)

Large-scale needlepoint stitch on canvas (petit point is the smallest). Gros point can be used for upholstery and cushions, as floor covering or as a hanging tapestry.

Ground color

The background color in fabrics, wallpaper, carpets or china.

Gueridon (Gay-ree-dohn)

A small French table with, ordinarily, a marble top, which can be used as either a cocktail table or an occasional table.

Guilloche (ghee-Yosh)

A repeating motif of equally spaced circles surrounded by a winding, interweaving band, first used in Greek architecture, then in furniture and moldings of the Italian Renaissance and the Louis XV and XVI periods. Today you can find it in carved wood moldings.

Hall porter chair

Also *guerite* (gay-*reet*), French for sentry box. A high-backed chair with a hood meant to protect the hall porter from the chilly drafts of lofty halls and corridors.

Hand-tufted carpet

A handmade cut-pile carpet woven like an Oriental, but of heavier wool with a much coarser texture.

Hard-surface flooring

All the rigid materials used to cover floors—hard and soft woods, brick, marble, flagstone, mosaic and ceramic tile. This includes the more resilient materials as well, such as rubber tile, linoleum, cork and vinyl.

Hardwood

Timber from broad-leafed trees: teak, walnut, mahogany, birch, beech, chestnut, oak, elm.

Harvest table

American provincial dining table, usually long and narrow, with one or two drop leaves.

Headboard

Part of the support structure of a bed, and, obviously, at the head. It can be anything from classical to contemporary, and made of any material from metal to cardboard, including upholstery.

Herringbone

A repeat pattern of chevrons in fabric, wood, stone or brickwork. (See the herringbone brick wall on page 27.)

Honan

The finest Chinese wild silk, which looks and feels like pongee.

Horn furniture

Originally found in hunting lodges, furniture made of horns and antlers became a collectors' pride. Queen Victoria and Theodore Roosevelt are said to have collected horn furniture, and it turns up today as chairs, sofas, tables, beds, étagères, chandeliers and mirrors.

Horsehair

A woven fabric that contains the hair from the mane and tail of horses. It was most popular as upholstery material in the Victorian era, is very durable and not particularly comfortable.

Hunt table

A sideboard table that can be rectangular or crescent-shaped and has drop leaves to augment the serving surface. Tall enough for people to stand around at hunt breakfasts, it is used today as a buffet, a desk, or lowered to serve as a cocktail table. If it has drawers, it's called a hunt board.

Hurricane lamp

So called because the candle is surrounded by a glass shade that makes it virtually hurricane-proof. Today they are used with candles, or wired for electricity and equipped with flame-shaped bulbs.

Hutch

A chest or cabinet on legs with an open shelf deck above, very popular as a sideboard in early American homes.

Imari

A Japanese porcelain elaborately decorated in just blue and white or in a combination of yellow, gold, green and red on a white ground and manufactured only for export. It has been copied by European porcelain makers such as Minton, Spode, Worcester and Derby. Imari is still being manufactured in Japan, but the new ware is not as refined and subtle as the antique pieces.

India print

An inexpensive cotton print, hand-blocked in bright colors, used mostly for bedspreads. I like to use them for wall coverings, curtains and upholstery.

Indirect lighting

Light from a concealed source reflected from a wall or ceiling to give a soft overall, almost shadowless illumination.

Inlay

A style of decorating in which materials of one kind —wood, ivory shell or metal—are set into the surface of another. The French and English cabinetmakers of the 18th century were masters of inlay, but the technique is still practiced.

Ironstone

White semi-porcelain china. Originally the clay contained slag from iron mines, which accounts for the name. Mason and Wedgwood ironstone are highly valued by collectors.

Jacobean

The style in favor during the reign of the Stuart kings James I and Charles I. The furniture was of oak heavily carved in the Baroque and Italian Renaissance tradition.

Jacobsen, Arne

Danish furniture designer, famous for his big "egg" chair, an upholstered chair of contoured plywood and steel.

Jacquard

Elaborately patterned damasks, brocades and tapestries woven on a loom invented by Joseph Marie Jacquard in 1801.

Japanning

A 17th-century technique of coating the surface of wood or metal with successive layers of oven-dried varnish.

Jardiniere (zhahr-deen-Yair)

A ceramic, metal or wood container for plants or flowers.

Joint stool

Jacobean low stool with turned and joined legs, usually not upholstered.

KD

Abbreviation for knock-down. This is furniture designed in parts and shipped unassembled to be put together by either the store that sells it or the customer who buys it. The cost of assembly and shipping is thus reduced and the final price consequently lower.

Knife edge

The single seam on a pillow or cushion, as opposed to a box edge, which has two seams with a space the thickness of the cushion between them.

Knole sofa

A completely upholstered sofa with back and sides of the same height and connected by knotted cords looped over wood finials in the corners. Sometimes the sides are hinged and can be let down, converting the sofa into a daybed. Said to be derived from a 17th-century sofa in Knole House, Kent, England.

Lacquer

A resin lac that hardens when exposed to air and can be polished to a mirror finish. To produce this furniture finish requires a slow and tedious buildup of layers of the lac. Real, hand-applied lacquer is truly beautiful and truly costly. Today's modern technology makes use of synthetics that rival the original and have the additional advantage of not being too susceptible to water stains and scratching.

Ladderback

A chair with horizontal slats like ladder rungs, typical of provincial and Early American furniture.

Lambrequin

A shaped valance—usually of fabric—which crowns a window and frames the sides as well. It can be used on beds, or even on chair backs.

Laminating

A process of bonding together thin layers of material. Plywood is so made. Formica and Micarta are plastics laminated to plywood. There are laminated plastic window shades, laminates for floors, and Japanese laminates of paper to form trays and bowls, all in a wide range of colors and textures.

Lapis lazuli

A semiprecious stone of a deep ultramarine blue that has been used decoratively since the days of Babylon. It was used for *objets de luxe* in the 18th century, combined with gold or malachite to create jewel boxes, urns, paperweights and such. The appearance of lapis can be simulated with paint, ceramic or printing on paper. It's very effective when used as a wall treatment, or as *faux lapis* on furniture.

Lavabo (lah-Vah-bow)

A hanging washbasin in two parts. The upper part contains water, while the lower is the basin. Sometimes it is mounted on a wood back, sometimes directly on the wall. Although originally intended for washing hands, today the lavabo is used as a planter or simply as a decorative accessory.

Lawson sofa

A completely upholstered sofa with a low, square back and flaring scroll arms.

Le Corbusier (1887–1965)

Enduringly influential Swiss architect, born Charles Edouard Jeanneret, who is responsible for some of the most controversial and inspired buildings of our time, and whose work included everything from furniture to the planned city of Chandigarh, India.

Lectern
A high stand, originally designed to support a church Bible, but now in general use to support any open book or small picture.

Leeds
Eighteenth-century English pottery, identifiable by its creamware, sometimes enameled, sometime pierced.

Library steps
Used in the 18th and 19th centuries to reach books on high library shelves, they were mostly tables or benches that concealed a ladder, sometimes with handrails. They are used today as display pieces for plants and accessories.

Library table (worktable)
A large double-pedestal table with drawers and, often, book space. I like to use library tables as worktables in almost any room, particularly as part of a grouping in the middle of the room or at right angles to a wall.

Linen fold
Carved paneling, originally Gothic, that looks like linen hanging in vertical folds.

Lit clos (lee clow)
Literally a closed bed—enclosed, that is, by wood paneling on three sides. Also called a cupboard bed.

Lit de repos (lee duh ru-Poh)
French version of the daybed, and meant as a spot to catch forty winks.

Loggia (Low-jah)
An open arcade or roofed gallery along one side of a room or a house.

Louis Philippe (loo-ee fee-Leap)
The revival of Louis XV styles during the reign of Louis Philippe (1830–48). A style often mistaken for Victorian.

Louis Quatorze (XIV) (loo-ee kah-Torz)
A Baroque furniture style emerging during the 17th century in France, distinguished by its sumptuous scale and symmetry, very masculine, very grand, the carving heavy and rich, the plain woods gilded and heavily ornamented. The famous cabinetmaker Boulle developed intricate marquetry of mother of pearl, bone, ivory, brass and tortoise shell. The chairs were covered in rich damasks, velvets and tapestries. Today this museum style is not very suitable for contemporary living, but I like the provincial or country interpretations. They work well in traditional, contemporary or mixed settings.

Louis Quinze (XV) (loo-ee kanze)
There are those who consider this the ultimate in design: very rococo and all curved lines, as in the curved cabriole leg. Decoration was rampant: marquetry, painting, lacquering, gilding and chinoiserie. Favored woods were native fruitwoods, mahogany and walnut along with veneers of more exotic rosewood, satinwood, amaranth and tulip. Today it is perhaps the most popular of all the French styles, in reproductions and adaptations. Again, I prefer the provincial interpretations, as being more livable.

Louis Seize (XVI) (loo-ee sayze)
This neoclassic style is, in its simplicity and restraint, very usable in today's settings. After the frills and fancies of Louis XV, cabinetmakers reacted with simple architectural forms derived from those that had recently come to light in the excavations of Pompeii and Herculaneum. Furniture became severe and straight-lined. Ornamentation was classic as well: egg and dart, palm leaves, laurel, fretwork, rinceaux, ribbons. Mahogany was the favorite wood, along with ebony, rosewood and tulip combined in marquetry. Striped satin and toiles were favored for upholstery fabrics.

Louvers
A series of slats designed to control light and air at both doors and windows. They may be horizontal or vertical, adjustable or stationary, made of metal, wood or plastic.

Lowestoft
Ceramic produced by a small porcelain factory in Lowestoft, England, from 1757 to 1802. The finer pieces are large punch bowls with painted Chinese and rococo designs inspired by the Oriental porcelains imported by the East India Company. Lowestoft is a favorite of collectors. It can be found not only in tableware, but in boxes, animal figures, mugs, tea

caddies and commemorative pieces, which are sometimes marked "A trifle from Lowestoft."

Macramé (mahk-rah-May)
French word for the hand-knotted fringe that the Turks introduced into Spain. It was used on Spanish rugs, bedspreads, shawls, curtains, pillows. Macramé is currently enjoying another spurt of popularity, and can even be used for screens and wall hangings.

Majolica
There are two types. Earliest is the 17th-century pottery with tin glaze and polychrome decoration that came from Italy, Spain and the Low Countries. A later, 19th-century type made in England, America and Europe is enamel-decorated white earthenware in natural animal, vegetable, fish and shell shapes.

Malachite
The czars used to decorate their palaces with this rich, yellow-green semi-precious stone. It's very hard to come by today, but its colors and patterns are duplicated in paint, vinyl and ceramic finishes.

Manmade fibers
Polymers—molecules in a chainlike structure—are the major component of most manmade fibers. Acetate and rayon are made of modified natural polymers; fiberglass from spun glass; polyacrylics, polyesters, polyurethanes and polyvinyls come from chemical compounds.

Marbleizing
The use of paint to make wood or metal look like marble. Sometimes—as in *faux marbre*—the effect is very real.

Marquetry
Inlay of contrasting materials: ivory, mother of pearl, etc.

Marquise (mahr-Keeze)
A French arm chair completely upholstered and wide enough to accommodate panniered skirts.

Medieval
Referring to the arts, architecture and furniture of the Middle Ages, which were characterized by beamed, vaulted ceilings and dark stained floors. I have used variations and adaptations of the medieval look in many of the country rooms I have done.

Mercury glass
Double-blown glass, the interior painted with silver nitrate, used for vases, epergnes, bowls and candlesticks, and effective in interiors where the glint of metal is required.

Mies van der Rohe, Ludwig (1886–1969)
Twentieth-century German-born architect, a director of the Bauhaus school, and probably most celebrated for the Seagram Building in New York City, designed with Philip Johnson. He created the first tubular-steel cantilevered chair as well as the celebrated Barcelona chair.

Millefleurs (meel-Fluhr)
"A thousand flowers" in French, used to describe an allover flower pattern, as in antique Chinese porcelains.

Ming yellow
The dazzling sulphur yellow of the glaze on Chinese porcelains of the Ming period. I particularly like using a Ming yellow vase as a color accent in a room —traditional or contemporary.

Miter (or mitre)
The joining of two sections of wood the edges of which have been cut at a 45-degree angle, so that they fit together at right angles. (See the section on beams, page 24.) Also the similar joining of two strips of molding in a picture frame, or striped fabric on ceilings, etc.

Modular furniture
Storage units based on standard modules that can be stacked or grouped in endless combinations.

Moiré (mwah-Ray)
A satiny and luxurious fabric with an apparent watermark that is created by twisting the weave or working the finished material on heated rollers.

Molding
A contoured strip of wood, stone, plaster, metal or plastic applied to woodwork, doors, windows, walls, ceilings or furniture.

Monochromatic color scheme
A color scheme that uses one color in various gradations together with black, white or a metallic gleam.

Montgolfier chair (mohng-goal-f'Yay)
A balloon-back chair designed by Georges Jacob for Louis XVI to commemorate the 1783 balloon ascent of the Montgolfier brothers.

Moustiers (mouse-t'Yay)
French faïence in soft greens and yellows, or blue and white, made in the factory of the same name founded in 1679.

Muffin stand
Any small tiered wood or metal stand, sometimes fitted with plates and designed for serving tea. Mostly used today for an hors d'oeuvre server or as an occasional table.

Mullion
The slender vertical upright that divides the glass panes of a window. In furniture it refers to the tracery on the glass-paned doors of a bookcase, secretary, etc.

Nailsea
Flasks, mugs, jugs, bottles, bowls, bells, canes, candlesticks, rolling pins and witch balls of colored glass made in Nailsea, England, from 1788 to 1873, with a random spattering of spots and splashes of white. Later styles alternated stripes of clear glass with pink and yellow.

Naugahyde
The U.S. Rubber Company's trademarked name for a vinyl upholstery material that closely resembles leather.

Navajo rugs
Wooden rugs made by the Navajo Indians of the American Southwest, according to a technique learned from the Spaniards. Originally the natural-color background was patterned with gray, black and white stripes. Later the Navajos extracted a red dye from tree bark and found sources for indigo. By the 19th century the familiar diamond and chevron patterns appeared. Handmade Navajo rugs are still being woven.

Needlepoint
A technique of cross-stitching a design in wool on canvas to produce an effect much like tapestry. There are various scales of needlepoint, the smallest being petit point, the largest, gros point.

Nelson, George
Contemporary American designer noted for his modular furniture designs, the most outstanding of which is a storage system hung from poles, by now quite a contemporary classic.

Neutrals
No-color colors that serve as background. Usually thought of are white, off white, ivory, but I consider camel a neutral, and certainly the many tones of wood.

Nevers (nay-Vare)
Decorative faïence noted for bold painted Persian and Chinese designs in opulent colors of Persian blue, purple and yellows, made in the town of Nevers in the 17th and 18th centuries.

Ninon
A sheer fabric of rayon, nylon or Dacron used for glass curtains.

Noguchi, Isamu
A major Japanese-American sculptor who has designed the charming and fanciful Akari paper lanterns as well as free-form furniture.

Numdah rugs
Accent rugs from Kashmir with bright hand embroidery on felt, usually in designs of flowers and birds. Small examples are occasionally used as saddle blankets.

Obelisk
A tall, four-sided stone Egyptian column that tapers toward the top. It has been adapted for domestic accessories such as clocks, barometers, thermometers and ornaments in metal, wood, semiprecious stones and contemporary crystal.

Objets d'art (ohb-jay Dar)
Literally objects of artistic worth: decorative accessories of superior quality.

Obsidian
Objets d'art were made of this glistening black volcanic glass during the French Empire period. Today you'll find it imitated in pressed glass.

Occasional tables
End tables, lamp tables, book tables, cocktail tables, tea tables and the like.

Ogee
The profile or side view of a molding made of two **S** curves meeting. Most often seen on top of pediments or on the lower edge of an apron.

Ombré (ohm-Bray)
A fabric design of graduated shades of one color, or rainbow-like gradations of many colors.

Opaline
An opalescent glass much in favor today, and very popular in the 19th century. It is found in a lovely blue, which is my favorite, but it's also available in white, pink and green. Antique opaline is very expensive, but a collectors' favorite.

Oriel
An oval bay window projecting from a wall and supported by a bracket.

Oriental rug
A rug of hand-woven or hand-knotted wool or silk, usually in an allover design, although there are examples in solid colors as well. The major types are Persian, Indian, Turkoman, Caucasian, Chinese and Turkish.

Ormolu (ohr-moh-Loo)
Gilded copper, bronze or brass ornaments or furniture mounts meant to look like gold.

Osnaburg
A modest, plain-weave, coarse cotton fabric resembling crash.

Overdoor
A decorative treatment over a doorway, originally designed as part of the architecture, but today, when most rooms are unadorned boxes, they can be added to a room in any number of moldings.

Overmantel
Any paneling or formal treatment of the chimney breast over a fireplace mantel.

Overscaled
Impressively proportioned furniture or patterns of unusually large size, used to achieve an effect of dominance.

Ovolo
A molding with a convex curve that resembles the wide inside curve of an eggshell. Usually painted or carved with the egg-and-dart pattern.

Pad foot
The end of a cabriole leg in Queen Anne furniture.

Painted furniture
A technique that goes back to the days of the Egyptians and reached its peak in 18th-century Europe, which completely obscures the natural grain of wood with an opaque finish of paint, enamel or lacquer. It can be either plain or decorated. Interpretations vary from country to country. The Venetians were masters of the painted finish. The English style, or japanning, was borrowed from the Orient, while some French furniture is done in pale pastels. I love painted furniture, from the deep rich colors of the French country style to the clear, bold lacquer finishes on contemporary Parsons tables.

Paisley
A fabric design that imitates the woven cashmere shawls first created at Paisley, Scotland, and is available in wallpaper, fabric, even vinyl.

Palampores
Resist-dyed or hand-painted cottons, chintzes and calicoes that predate the invention of block printing.

Palladian
The unique neoclassical architectural style created by Andrea Palladio, a 16th-century Italian architect. The Palladian window is a hallmark of 18th-century New England architecture.

Paneling
Decorative detail on furniture, doors, and particularly on walls and ceilings.

Panetière (pahn-uh-T'yere)
A French open and carved box for displaying bread. In today's homes it is used as an end table or a storage piece.

Panné (pahn-Nay)
Pile fabric, either velvet or satin, with the pile pressed back to give a lustrous finish.

Pargework (pargetry)
The art (nearly lost) of applying stucco or plaster to a flat surface to create a design in relief. Today many of the classic architectural designs have been copied in anaglypta, which can be attached to a wall or ceiling with adhesive.

Parquet (pahr-Kay)
Wood inlaid in geometric shapes for floors and even furniture. *Parquet de Versailles* was a basket-weave pattern originally used for floors of the Grand Trianon, and now used as a pattern for tabletops.

Parsons table
Named for the Parsons School of Design, where it originated, this now classic square or rectangular table with apron and legs the same width is found in a great variety of finishes and in almost every size, from low cocktail tables to console and dining tables. You'll see many, many uses of the Parsons table in the photographs in this book.

Passementerie (pahss-mahn-Tree)
French term for all kinds of trimmings: braid, tapes, ribbons, gimp, tinsel and beads.

Patchwork
This popular fabric technique didn't start in colonial America. The Egyptians did it first—piecing bits of fabric together and then quilting them—but it became a true decorative art in America in the 18th and 19th centuries.

Patina
A surface that is mellowed by age, wear and rubbing. It's found on very fine old pieces of furniture—or bronze—but can be achieved artificially.

Peachblow
A 19th-century American art glass made to imitate Chinese peach bloom porcelain. Colors range from red, rose, soft pink, to white, light blue and even a greenish yellow.

Peacock chair
Sometimes called a Saratoga or cobra chair, and noted for its high fan back that swells out like the hood of a cobra. The originals came from Hong Kong and were made of rattan, and the chair has been popular since the Victorian days.

Pedestal
A substitute support for the legs of a chair or table, a pedestal can be either square, rectangular, round or oval. Without a top it can serve as a support for a vase of flowers or a piece of sculpture. I like pedestals in all manner of materials: wood, mirror, chrome, clear or white plexiglass, marble or even terra cotta, and I like to light pedestals from within when they're made of translucent plexiglass.

Pediment
An architectural triangle over a window, door, portico, the outdoor gable of a house, or used as the crowning element of a cabinet. Sometimes it is "broken," or interrupted, sometimes rounded.

Pelmet
A short valance or cornice that covers or conceals a curtain rod.

Pembroke table
Originally designed by Chippendale as a breakfast table and named by Hepplewhite for the Earl of Pembroke, the 18th-century original had two drop leaves supported by brackets that pull out from the apron. Today they are used for lamp tables or small worktables in small-scale room groupings.

Petit point
The smallest stitch of the needlepoint family.

Pewter
An alloy of lead and tin in a dull gray that can be either polished or left mat. Although originally devised as a substitute for silver, antique pewter can command a higher price today than silver.

Pickling
A technique which changes the complexion of wood by the rubbing of white paint into the grain.

Piece-dying
Some fabrics are woven of threads that have been dyed before weaving—or yarn-dyed. When instead the woven fabric is dyed, it is called piece-dying.

Pied-de-biche (p'yed-duh-Bish)
The deer's hoof at the end of a slightly curved leg—the parent of the cabriole leg.

Pier glass
A tall wall mirror of the Victorian era that was usually hung between big windows or over a low console. Originally the pier glass was meant to stand on the floor against a wall.

Pierced panels
Wood, stone, even plastic worked in open designs, usually thought of as Oriental, Spanish or Moorish.

Pierced panels can be used at windows, as doors or as room dividers.

Pilaster
A half-round or rectangular column applied to a wall as architectural detail.

Pile fabrics
Fabrics of any fiber—natural or synthetic—that have a pile texture. These can be terry cloth, plush, velour, velvet or frieze.

Piping
A cord trim covered with fabric that finishes and conceals the seams of upholstery, slipcovers, draperies and cushions.

Piqué
A heavy cotton fabric that looks quilted—hence the French name. Another piqué is a decorative inlay of shell, ivory or mother of pearl that appears on small 17th- and 18th-century objects such as jewel and snuff boxes.

Plate rail
A functional piece of architecture that allows for a display of china above eye level.

Plinth
Architectural term for the block of wood or stone at the base of a column. Today this can be of any material and used as a base for sculpture.

Plywood
The product of a special process that glues together several layers (or plies) of wood—the grain of one ply at right angles to the grain of the ply next to it. This stacking of grains produces a wood that is a good deal stronger than solid wood.

Point d'Hongrie (Pwan dong-Gree)
An eggplant upholstery fabric in needlepoint flame stitch on silk.

Polyester fibers
Manmade fibers that have nearly endless applications in fabrics. (Dacron is one of the numerous trademarked names for polyester fibers.) When used in combination with a natural fiber such as cotton, a "permanent press" condition can be created which gives the blended fabric enduring crispness.

Pongee
Raw silk fabric in a natural light tan. Though originally produced in China, pongee has been fabricated of manmade fibers as well.

Pot table (poh tab'l)
The original night table, usually tubular in shape, with an interior shelf, a door and a marble top on which was placed a bedside oil lamp. Today it can be used as an end table or lamp table in a traditional setting.

Poudreuse (poo-Druhz)
Also called a vanity, this is a French table with a mirror used by milady for applying makeup.

Pre-Columbian
Arts and artifacts of the Indian cultures of Mexico, South and Central America pre-dating the discovery of the New World by Columbus.

Prie-dieu (pree-d'Yuh)
A low stool for kneeling while at prayer. Now used to refer to a chair with a high back, a low seat and a narrow shelf, rail or pad across the top that can be used as an armrest or headrest.

Psychedelics
Luminous colors and bold prints in swirling designs that create the appearance of motion.

Pull-up chair
A small lightweight open-arm chair with tapered legs that can be easily moved from one place in the room to another.

Quarry tile
Unglazed paving tile or stone that can be had in a multitude of sizes, shapes and colors.

Quarter round
A molding with a profile of one-quarter circle.

Quartz
A transparent mineral found in hexagonal crystals. The most common is clear rock crystal, but there are others: Smoky brown, heliotrope and bloodstone; red, opaque jasper, banded sardonyx and onyx; bluish violet amethystine, pale yellow, false topaz or citrine.

Quatrefoil
A Gothic decorative design composed of four touch-

ing circles and looking much like a four-leaf clover.

Quattrocento (kwat-roh-Chen-toh)
Early Italian Renaissance, 1400–1500, a transitional period from Gothic to classic revival. Typical pieces are the credenza, the Savonarola chair, the Dante chair and the sgabello, a wooden side chair either with three legs or with carved wood slabs at the front and back.

Quimper (kam-Pair)
French faïence made near the town of Quimper which is provincial in feeling, with peasant scenes on bright yellow backgrounds.

Rabbet
A cabinet door is rabbeted to take a panel; the side rails of a bed are rabbeted to accommodate the box spring and mattress.

Rafraichissoir (ray-fray-shee-Swar)
A "refresher" or bar cart of the time of Louis XV, used for chilling wine, its top fitted with tole or iron bottle holders. Underneath were shelves for extra dishes and glasses. In modern use, the bottles are usually replaced by plants.

Reading table
A small 18th-century table with an adjustable top that holds a book. Probably derived from a lectern, which it resembles.

Récamier (reh-kah-m'Yeh)
A French Empire chaise longue with the head much higher than the foot, named for Madame Récamier (who is seen reclining on one in the painting by David).

Reeding
Parallel lengthwise beads on, for example, the Louis XVI tapered leg. (See fluting.)

Refectory table
Originally a long, low table, supported by heavy stretchers, used in the dining area, or refectory, of a monastery. Later the table was shortened and fitted with pull-out leaves, to become the first self-contained expansion table.

Renaissance (1500–1700)
The first of the European styles to reflect Greek and Roman forms.

Rendering
A drawing of a proposed decorating plan prepared by a designer to show a client as nearly as possible how a completed room will look.

Rep
An upholstery and drapery fabric with a distinct rib woven into the fabric.

Repoussé (ruh-poos-Say)
Decorative sheet metal work in relief achieved by hammering the design into the metal from the back.

Reproductions
Copies of old pieces, exactly duplicating the originals, even to the finish and patina. Today the word is often loosely applied to pieces that derive their flavor from older models but are produced in different materials and proportions.

Restoration
Used of houses, rooms, china or furniture that have been restored to their original condition.

Riser
The upright section of a stair step that connects adjoining treads.

Rockingham
Eighteenth-century English pottery with an uneven glaze of deep brown. In the 19th century the original Rockingham factory began to create decorative porcelains in brilliant ground colors—from dinner services to large vases, figures and incense burners shaped like quaint cottages, a design copied later by Staffordshire.

Rococo
A style of decoration that reached its zenith in 18th-century Europe, particularly during the reign of Louis XV. Rocailles and coquilles (rock and shell motifs—thus the term) were used in profusion on carved and painted ornaments.

Roman shade
A variation on the Austrian shade. The folds of flat fabric panels are accordion-pleated horizontally rather than being shirred in scallops. The effect is much more tailored than the opulent look of the Austrian shade.

Romanesque
An ecclesiastical style of art and architecture that

prevailed in Europe from about 800 to 1100 A.D., after the collapse of the Roman Empire, and eventually evolved into Gothic. Today many Romanesque influences can be seen in designs of rugs, fabrics and wallpaper. There is a vigor to the period that works well in contemporary rooms.

Room divider
A partition that separates areas of a room, be it a built-in storage wall, sliding panels, a line of furniture in a grouping, a folding screen or a decorative fabric hung from the ceiling.

Rosenthal
China firm established in Bavaria in 1879, which continues to manufacture procelains in modern shapes, designs and colors. Within the last few years Rosenthal has branched out into silverware, glassware and stainless steel.

Rosette
A disk of leaves arranged in the form of a rose as a decorative motif on furniture, fabrics, wallpapers and architecture.

Rustic furniture
Pieces in which, for example, real branches and limbs of trees form the legs, arms and backs of chairs or the components of tables.

Saarinen, Eero (1910–61)
The architect and designer celebrated for certain famous buildings as well as the mushroom pedestal table and chairs and the lounge chair of molded plastic and foam rubber on a metal rod base that is manufactured and distributed by Knoll Associates.

Sang de Boeuf (sahng duh buff)
Literally ox blood. The Chinese porcelain glaze color developed during the Kang Hsi period (1662–1722).

Santo
A carved and painted image of the Virgin Mary, Joseph, the infant Jesus or any of the Christian saints made in countries where Spanish colonial and Catholic influence has come to bear—Mexico, Puerto Rico, the Philippines, South America.

Savonarola chair (sah-voh-neh-Row-lah)
Italian Renaissance chair made of curved interlacing slats in an X shape with a carved wood back.

Savonnerie (sah-vohn-err-Ree)
French rug and tapestry factory producing hand-woven high-pile wool rugs in pastel colors and floral and scroll patterns for 18th- and 19th-century palaces. The originals are very costly, but they have been imitated at more modest prices.

Sawbuck table
A large table of Gothic design with two X-shaped supports. Originally made of wood, but today sawbuck tables are made of steel or chrome with glass, lucite or marble tops.

Scagliola (kah-l'yee-Oh-lah)
Hard plaster surface embedded with pieces of granite, alabaster, marble or other stones, then highly polished, used for the tops of tables or chests.

Scale
Size and proportion of a piece relative to its surroundings and other elements in a room. Furniture with skinny, low lines are "lightly scaled," and pieces that are bigger and more massive are heavy in scale.

Scallop
The scallop shell, one of the most conspicuous motifs of Renaissance, Queen Anne and Chippendale furniture.

Sconce
A lighting fixture attached to a wall, holding a candle or oil lamp or electric bulb, that is not only a source of light but a decorative element as well.

Scrim
A loose, open cotton fabric that has been used for years in theatre hangings for scenic effects, and is now popular and effective as a glass curtain.

Second Empire
Period of the reign of Napoleon III (1852–70). The furnishings of the period resembled the Victorian, but tended to be more frivolous. Typical examples are furniture of mother of pearl, papier-mâché and opaline glass.

Selvage
The reinforced outer edge of fabric or vertical margin of wallpaper.

Shantung
A heavy pongee fabric of wild silk, cotton or a blend

of both, useful for curtains, bedspreads and even upholstery.

Sheffield plate
Eighteenth-century English silver plate made by fusing copper and silver, and shaped into all sorts of utility pieces, such as candle snuffers, teapots, trays. In old and well-used pieces the copper shows through the silver, and collectors never have them replated.

Shoji
Japanese word for translucent sliding wood-framed panel screens used for partitioning rooms.

Sideboard
The 16th-century serving table that ultimately became a chest, cabinet, hutch or cupboard with open shelves above and drawers below. Today the sideboard is usually a simple shelf table without storage space.

Sisal
Natural fiber made from the leaves of the agave plant from Mexico, Central America, the West Indies and Africa.

Sleigh bed
American interpretation of a French Empire bed, so called because the high, scrolled ends look like the front of a sleigh.

Slip seat
A removable upholstered seat that slips into and out of the framework of a chair so that it can be easily removed and recovered.

Slipware
Pottery decorated on the unfired surface with slip— a clay that has the consistency of batter. The technique consists of tracing the slip on the piece with a brush to form a pattern, or else coating the entire surface with slip and then scratching the design through the coating so that the underlying clay color can be seen. The latter technique is called sgraffito.

Sofa table (console table)
A late 18th-century oblong table with a drop leaf, said to have been designed by Thomas Sheraton to be used in front of a sofa. I find today's console table useful behind a sofa, in the center of a room as a worktable and part of a center grouping, or against a wall with an important mirror or painting above it to form a major balance point in a room.

Soffit
The underside of a projecting cornice, beam or wide molding.

Soft-paste porcelain
A type of 17th-century European porcelain. Soft-paste porcelain was compounded of fused ground glass and clay and took more subtle colorations than true porcelain. Unfortunately the glaze scratched easily.

Soupière (soo-p'Yehr)
Originally a soup tureen with platter and cover. In furniture the term means pedimented tops of beds, cabinets, chairs, etc.

Soutache (soo-Tasch)
Round, narrow braid in a herringbone design used for edging or trimming fabric.

Spice chest
A chest with many small drawers used, as the name implies, for holding spices.

Spindle back
Chair back constructed in a series of slender, vertical turned members—typical of Windsor chairs.

Spode
Creamware and bone china produced by the Spode factories in England.

Spool turning
A turning for table legs and bed frames that came about with the invention of the power lathe. The name is explicit—a cylindrical piece of wood that looks like a stack of spools.

Staffordshire
Pottery manufactured by many factories in Staffordshire, England. Original Staffordshire figures are collectors' items. The most familiar is the pug dog design.

Stoneware
Any non-porous, hard-clay pottery excluding porcelain. There are fine antique examples dating back to 7th-century China, but the technique is still practiced today in contemporary shapes and designs.

Storage wall
A free-standing or built-in collection of closets, cabinets, chests or shelves used for all manner of storage.

There are modern prefabricated versions, stacking units, pole-supported units or wall-hung constructions.

Stretch fabrics
Knit or woven fabrics of either natural or synthetic yarns used for upholstery or slipcovers on contoured furniture. They do just what the name implies—stretch to fit what's underneath.

Stretcher
The horizontal support that braces the legs of chairs and tables. There are many styles, each typical of its period, from Windsor and Pembroke down to the most contemporary.

Table chair
A 10th-century dual-purpose chair that serves as both a table and a chair. When the hinged top is down it's a table—when up, it forms the chair back and the supports serve as arms.

Taffeta
A closely woven fabric of cotton, silk or manmade fibers that is smooth and lustrous on both sides. Usually used for bedspreads, slipcovers, draperies, and in some cases to upholster small chairs.

Tansu chest
A Japanese chest containing several drawers, and characterized by an antique red finish and black metal hardware. Tansu chests can be used singly or in groups for storage, but are equally effective as end tables, lamp tables and cocktail tables. They are also made in a variety of exotic woods from the Orient.

Tapestry
Originally a hand-woven fabric of linen, wool or silk used as a wall hanging or for upholstery. Most tapestry fabrics now are machine-made.

Tatami
Mats of rice straw and rushes, three feet by six feet, and bound with cloth tape, used by the Japanese as all-purpose floor and mattress covering.

Tavern table
A low, rectangular table with square or turned legs, intended for dining and drinking in 17th-century taverns. Today a tavern table might be used as a dining table or worktable in a traditional country setting.

Tea table
The popularity of tea in Europe in the 17th century brought forth a great spate of small tables for serving tea which can be used today as occasional tables or cocktail tables.

Templet (template)
A pattern or outline drawing of a decorative element or piece of furniture which can be used for placement in scale drawings and floor plans.

Tent ceiling
During the French Empire this was a technique for imitating the top of a tent as a ceiling treatment.

Terra cotta
A clay that varies in color from light buff to deep red, used for figurines, reliefs, floor tiles and garden statuary.

Terrazzo (tehr-Raht-zoh)
A hard surface material for floors and walls, made of a mixture of ground chips of marble and cement and highly polished.

Tête de nègre (tait duh naygr')
A decorator's color—literally "Negro head"—that is a deep brown-black with a hint of purple.

Thai silks
Silk fabrics from Thailand in a glorious range of solid colors or patterns, weights and weaves. I love them for upholstery, pillow covers, draperies and bed hangings.

Theatrical gauze
An inexpensive, transparent, loosely woven linen or cotton fabric, heavily sized to give it body and available in a wide range of colors. Long used for scenic effects in the theatre, it is now used in interior design—usually for glass curtains.

Thonet, Michael (1796–1871)
Designer of bentwood furniture, who developed a method of steaming birch wood and molding it into curving shapes along rococo lines. The Thonet rocker is much copied.

Ticking
A strong, heavy cotton fabric woven in stripes, patterns and plain, used to cover mattresses and as wall covering, slipcovers and curtains.

Tieback
Cord, fabric bands or ornamental devices for holding curtains back at the sides.

Toile de Jouy (twahl duh zhoo-Ee)
Toile is the French word for a finely woven cotton fabric, and a toile de Jouy is printed with classical scenes, ordinarily on a white or off-white ground. These classical cotton prints first appeared in the 18th century, and continue to be popular today.

Tole
Shaped and painted tin or other metal that is used for decorative objects such as lamps, chandeliers, trays, boxes and even occasional tables.

Tongue and groove
A type of joint used for flooring, paneled walls and doors. A narrow projection, or tongue, of one board fits exactly into a groove, or rabbet, in another.

Topiary
The centuries-old garden art of trimming and training trees and shrubs into the shapes of animals, people, birds or geometric forms. Now topiary designs have found their way into fabric and wallpaper prints.

Tortoise shell
The shell from sea turtles used as a veneer or inlay material. In Renaissance Italy mirror frames, tables and boxes were covered with tortoise shell veneers. André Charles Boulle, in the reign of Louis XIV, was noted for his superb marquetry in tortoise shell and brass. Real tortoise is rare and costly, but it is widely imitated in paper, paint and plastic.

Travertine
A light beige limestone from Italy, with a surface that has irregularities and imperfections, used for floors, walls and tabletops. Often imitated in vinyl.

Tray ceiling
A ceiling with sloping sides that looks very much like an inverted tray. This construction tends to make a room look loftier, and also helps air circulation.

Treen work
Turned and shaped wooden objects, mostly 19th-century, and made either by hand or on a lathe. There are many shapes in treen work, from miniature fruit to boxes, bowls and epergnes.

Treillage (tray-Yahzh)
Not to be confused with the regular garden trellis, this is an elaborate arrangement of thin, crisscrossed wood slats, used indoors and out in the 18th century, that has a period feeling but can be very contemporary as well.

Trestle table
Primitive table made by laying boards across trestles or horses (and taking them away when not in use). In the Middle Ages the trestles were attached to the boards.

Trictrac table
Seventeenth-century table with a removable top that exposed a board for either backgammon or chess.

Trim
The interior woodwork of a room, such as window frames, chair rails, cornices, molding, etc.

Trivet
A metal stand or table with either three or four legs, originally used for warming dishes by the fire but suitable as plant stands or occasional tables.

Trompe l'oeil (trohmp l'oiy)
Literally "to fool the eye." Paint or paper can be used to fake a building, a view of garden or sea, or a material other than the actual one—such as marble, wood, drapery, etc.

Trumeau (trew-Moh)
A French combination mirror with a painting or carving over it. In the 18th century a trumeau was built into the overmantel or into the paneling between two windows.

Trundle bed
A low bed on casters that would roll or trundle under a full-sized bed when not in use. There are many contemporary versions—particularly in furniture for children's rooms.

Turning
Any wood piece turned and shaped on a lathe—as chair legs, table pedestals, bedposts, stair balustrades.

Tussah silk
Coarse, beige-colored silk that comes from the wild Asiatic silkworm. This is the raw material from which

are made pongee, shantung, shiki silk and the nubby tussah fabrics.

Tuxedo sofa
American sofa with back and arms of the same height. Can be completely upholstered or have a visible wooden frame.

Twist turning
Spiral turning that looks like a twisted strand of rope or hawser, used since the 17th century in decorative columns and cabinetwork. The double twist looks like two ropes twined together.

Umber
Earth-brown pigment that is used to give white paint a "gray" or antique shade. Burnt umber is calcinated and has a reddish color.

Underglaze
Decoration or color on china, applied before glazing.

Vaisselier (vay-seh-L'yeh)
French version of the Welsh dresser. A low cabinet with open shelves and racks above them, complete with guardrails, to store and display china.

Valance
Wood, metal or drapery used across the top of a window treatment or over a canopied bed.

Vallauris (vahl-loh-Rhee)
Of the pottery made in the town of Vallauris since the 19th century, the best known are the superb designs by Picasso.

Vargueno (vahr-Gayn-yoh)
A 16th- and 17th-century Spanish drop-front cabinet desk, usually set on a table or chest. The cabinet contains many drawers and is equipped with side handles for carrying.

Velour
A classification of upholstery-weight fabrics—of silk, linen, cotton or synthetic fibers—that have a pile.

Velvet
A general term for all warp-pile fabrics, with the exception of terry.

Veneer
A thin layer of wood applied to a solid base to give the appearance of a more costly or fancier wood. Veneers can also be in tortoise shell, pearl, ivory, marble or other materials.

Vermeil (vehr-May)
Gilded bronze or silver, used as a substitute for solid gold. Originally an outright fake adopted by the profligate kings of France to simulate gold, but today an admired alternative to silver in table flatware, for example.

Vernis martin (vehr-Nee mahr-Tan)
A varnish with great depth and brilliance, although not so durable as lacquer.

Vitrine (vee-Treen)
A piece for the display and storage of china and objets d'art. Usually a cabinet with glass doors and, sometimes, glass top and sides as well.

Volute
A three-dimensional spiral scroll from the Greek Ionic order used in furniture decoration and drawer pulls.

Wainscot
Geometrically designed paneling that goes only partway up a wall and is sometimes topped by a plate rail or chair rail.

Wale
The ribs or cords in fabrics like corduroy, which is described as pin-wale, or wide-wale. The wale can also be a series of loops that run lengthwise in a knitted fabric like tricot.

Warp
The yarns that run lengthwise in a fabric, interwoven with the filling yarn or woof.

Warp print
Fabric woven with a plain filling, or woof, on a printed warp to give the surface a watery, shadowed look.

Waterford
Cut glass, produced since the 18th century in Waterford, Ireland, used not only for table glasses but for chandeliers and sconces as well.

Wedgwood
One of the greatest English potteries, founded in the 18th century by Josiah Wedgwood. Original Wedg-

wood was inspired by the 18th-century archaeological discoveries at Pompeii and Herculaneum and took its forms from classical antiquity. Jasperware, basaltware and queen's ware are the best-known Wedgwood, and jasperware was used not only for decorative objects but as panels on walls and mantels. Manufactured today in table services, urns and vases, lamp bases, etc., the patterns and colors are also reproduced in fabrics and wallpaper.

Welsh dresser
A cabinet with a base closed by drawers or doors and a top with open shelves for the storage and display of china.

Welting
Lengths of cotton cord covered in fabric and sewn between upholstery and slipcover seams to give them strength and a more finished look. Also known as piping.

Wicker
Any airy, woven furniture of natural or synthetic fibers such as reed, rattan, willow, even twisted paper.

William and Mary (1689–1702)
The style of English furniture made during the reign of Mary Stuart and William of Orange, her Dutch husband. Furniture of this period takes its richness from Louis XIV, but is scaled down to fit more intimate rooms. Legs were turned and braced with serpentine stretchers and the Dutch club foot and scroll leg foretold the Queen Anne cabriole leg. Chairs were often covered with needlepoint. Walnut was used, with much veneering and marquetry, and finished with lacquer and japanning. Original pieces of this period are rare, but the style is often copied.

Windsor chair
Named after Windsor Castle in England, this chair first appeared during the reign of Queen Anne. The originals were made by wheelwrights, who laced the bentwood back frames with spindles for support and pegged legs into the saddle-shaped seats. Variations include comb, the hoop, the fan, the bow and the rocking chair.

Woof
Also weft or filling. The yarns that run from selvage to selvage at right angles to the warp yarns.

Writing table
A flat-topped desk with a row of drawers or compartments in the apron, and sometimes with pull-out leaves at the side.